W9-ABX-544

The Secret Life of Teens

Young People Speak Out About Their Lives

Edited by

Gayatri Patnaik and

Michelle T. Shinseki

With a Foreword by the Producers of www.bolt.com

The world's most popular Web site for college and high school students

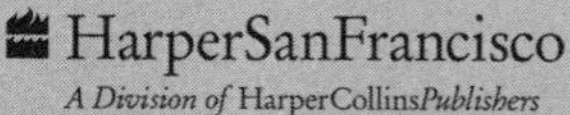

HarperSanFrancisco
A Division of HarperCollins*Publishers*

HarperCollins books may be purchased for educational, business, or sales promotional use. For information please write: Special Markets Department, HarperCollins Publishers, 10 East 53rd Street, New York, NY 10022.

HarperCollins Web site: http://www.harpercollins.com

FIRST EDITION

Library of Congress Cataloging-in-Publication Data

The secret life of teens: young people speak out about their lives / edited by Gayatri Patnaik and Michelle T. Shinseki. — 1st ed.

p. cm.

Includes index.

ISBN 0-688-1707-65 (pbk.)

1. Teenagers—Conduct of life. I. Patnaik, Gayatri. II. Shinseki, Michelle T.

BJ1661 .S43 2000

30521.—dc35 00-035050

---

01 02 03 04 ❖RRD(H) 10 9 8 7 6 5 4

For Aditya, Arun, Maya, & Uday

—GP

For my parents in this world
And for Grandma Shinseki in the next one

—MTS

Contents

WHAT TEENS KNOW

Who I Am and Who I'll Be

TO TEENS FROM TEENS

LOOKING AHEAD

Doing Our Part

PART TWO: INFLUENCES

Friendship

The Heart

Religion

Race

Teachers

PART THREE: PASSAGES

Sexuality

ON VIRGINITY

GETTING PHYSICAL

GAY/LESBIAN

ON MOTHERHOOD

Divorce

Death

DEATH OF A FRIEND

Substance Abuse

SMOKING

ALCOHOL

DRUGS

Assault and Harassment

SEXUAL ABUSE

PHYSICAL ABUSE

Stepparents

Siblings

Grandparents

Parents

Acknowledgments

First and foremost, we are grateful to all the contributors who grace these pages. By sharing your convictions, your anxieties, and your dreams, you have given the world precious snapshots of teen hearts at the millennium.

Thousands of submissions came in for this book, and, regrettably, we couldn't use them all. We wish to acknowledge each of you who submitted a letter because every single one made a difference and has influenced the course of this book.

Bolt.com, the largest teenage destination in the cyberworld, reaches over three million teens every month all across the world. The producers of this unique Web site were the conduit for some moving letters we received, and we applaud their commitment to teenagers today.

Tanya McKinnon, our agent at Mary Evans, Inc., has been an inspiration from the beginning. Joann Davis, our publisher, has been the guiding light for this project. Joann was our biggest cheerleader, and her commitment to the project, and to us, made all the difference.

With efficiency, expertise and humor, the folks at Harper San Francisco—especially Renee Sedliar—greatly eased the challenging task of producing this book.

A handful of friends provided constant support, for which we are grateful: Samantha Jane Altea, Kristina Hokenberg, Elena Megaro, Cindy Nastanski, Elizabeth Puccini, Sarah Zimmerman, and especially Licia Fiol-Matta—thank you!

Foreword

Getting to know teenagers is what we do at Bolt.com. We're the biggest Web site in the world for teens, with over three million of them visiting the site every month. In fact, teens write almost all of our content—plus chat, post on the message boards, keep on-line diaries, send notes, and more.

Through Bolt, we've seen amazing instances of teens connecting with one another as they share their own stories and check out others'. Every day, countless light bulbs switch on: "I'm not alone!" But while teens themselves may be more connected to one another, we adults remain as clueless as ever. True, teens today face many of the same issues their parents faced—dealing with sex, college applications, peer pressures—but there are also significant differences.

For one thing, they're more savvy than their parents were, thanks to increased access to information, with hundreds of channels on satellite television, a cavalcade of teen magazines, and the mighty Internet. This has both negative and positive implications. On the one hand, as we enter this new millennium, a high school student need only plug in her PlayStation to interact with material traditionally thought of as "for mature audiences only." On the other hand, a decade ago, an American high school student might barely have heard of Tunisia, while today, a sixteen-year-old Texan could well consider a sixteen-year-old Tunisian one of his best friends—even though they've only corresponded via e-mail and never met in real life. For better or worse, yesterday's boundaries are being broken down.

And, not surprisingly, teens are growing up faster. When something like the shooting in Littleton, Colorado, occurs, teenagers' hearts can't help but get a bit heavier and a bit harder. Meanwhile, adults suddenly realize that teens aren't all the young innocents that we thought they were. Realizing the horrors a few are capable of, we "protect" the rest with curfews, school dress codes, locker searches, and so on. No longer trusted as just kids, teens ironically find themselves treated more like children than ever. Unfortunately, adults often make negative assumptions about teenagers we don't know—and even those we do. We love to point fingers and pontificate about why teen violence or drug use among teens is happening and what we need to do as a society to fix it. But how often do we ask teens themselves what *they* think about the issues that directly affect them? How often do we ask for *their* sides of the story?

This is why *The Secret Life of Teens* is so groundbreaking. As adults, we're obviously missing something—and the teens who have written the letters here are filling us in. As it turns out, teens have a lot of intelligent and insightful comments on just about everything. The letters here have captured the vital issues of our time, from drugs to divorce to dating, from God to guns to being gay. And the beauty is that they're not written by so-called experts on the teen condition. They're testimonies by the *real* experts—teens themselves—who are in a better position to tell us their secrets than anyone else.

The Secret Life of Teens is about listening. It's about finding out what's really important to the young people who are already shaping the world they will inherit. And ultimately, it's about listening to and investing in our future.

JANE MOUNT
Executive Producer
www.bolt.com

LISSA HURCHALLA
Content Director
www.bolt.com

Introduction

A close friend called me several weeks ago with disturbing news: he had found his son unconscious in his bedroom the week before. I was speechless and completely unprepared for a revelation of this sort. As far as I knew, my friend had a good family life. There had never been a hint that something was amiss with his son. My mind searched desperately for reasons: A medical condition no one was aware of? A love relationship gone wrong? A drug overdose? An attempt at suicide? I had last seen his son six months ago, and he had seemed well—healthy, well adjusted, and self-confident.

After a brief trip to the emergency room, my friend's son was fine, with no permanent damage done. But the shock was still apparent in my friend's voice. "He was experimenting with some strange cocktail of drugs," he explained to me, haltingly.

They were the last family I expected this to happen to. The episode served as a wake-up call for both of us, coming as it did completely out of the blue. Who would have suspected Derek was experimenting with drugs?

WHAT WE FOUND

As editors of this book, we approached this project suspecting that, like many adults, we had only a cursory understanding of the teen heart at the millennium. And we were right. Our goal had been to help create a forum for young people—a safe place for them to express themselves on their own terms. We had no idea how they might respond or, indeed, even if they would. But they did—and in astounding numbers. This generation of young men and women stepped unabashedly forward, presenting us with nearly five thousand vignettes about the most private aspects of their lives. They confessed and communicated, ranted and rejoiced, and instructed and inspired.

Perhaps the quickest thing they established was that while we adults might think we understand teenagers, we don't. And lest we succumb to the sentimental temptation of comparing them to our own teen selves, we should be forewarned: it might not take us very far. In Steve's memorable words, "Listen, if any 'elders' are reading this—get a clue, we're not you!"

Letter after letter requests that adults stop falling for sensationalistic media depictions characterizing teens as gun-toting and substance-abusing delinquents. As Bryan states, "Not all teens are sex–crazed–evil–doing maniacs." Young people have caught onto a certain us-versus-them mentality and, as Angela indicates, is capable of turning the tables on us quite effectively: "The 'grown-ups' of the world point a lot of fingers at us. They say our generation will be the end of the future, but if you look long enough, you'll see we're not running the world yet, and it is still going to hell!"

This is clearly a generation that recognizes its own worth and will protest being disparaged. And if their defensiveness is occasionally apparent, so is their pain. Jae addresses a letter to "the teenagers of the world who feel alone" and confesses, "I was a cutter. The technical term is self-mutilation or self-injury, but you can call it whatever you want." Mandy writes of "the taunts in the classroom, the jeers in P.E., and the superbeautiful people" who "laugh and point and snicker" at those who are physically larger than what society deems a desirable weight. Alissa similarly notes our "cultural obsession with weight" and writes, "I am haunted by the gaping ravine between the image I want to obtain and the misshapen one that appears to me in the mirror every morning."

Apart from expressions of rage and frustration at society's unreasonable standards for beauty, this generation intends to confront the adult world about other aspects of its legacy. And if we didn't mention that they are unequivocal in their demand that we listen, Torea's words will help us all remember: "Finally. The perfect opportunity to confront you. And there is no way that you can walk away now. You must listen to and accept these brutal truths."

One brutal truth is divorce or, as they say, thanks for "dropping the big D-bomb on us." While many letters sadly acknowledge Maureen's observation that ultimately "happiness does not always mean togetherness," scores of letter writers testified to intense trauma resulting from the physical, and often emotional, absence of one parent after a divorce. Torea's letter is similar to many that we read; she juxtaposes the halcyon days of her youth with her father's current indifference, warning: "Dad, you'll regret this someday. Maybe not today. Maybe not tomorrow. Perhaps not until we are both very, very old."

But what remains awe inspiring about this generation is its resolve, its resiliency, and its clarity. Sabrina addresses a man she "no longer considers a father," noting all the sacrifices he made the family undergo while behaving hypocritically. Sabrina informs him, "Despite your beliefs, you are not perfect," and adds, piercingly, "how could you have been so selfish?" And

Jessica's promise to an emotionally absent parent was echoed time and again through many of our letters: "I'm going to be someone—with or without you."

This generation's impressive tenacity is matched only by its commitment to improving the future. Mia addresses her letter to "future fathers," and after recounting her own poignant story pleads with future fathers to remember that "your children need you."

And did we mention that this generation will no longer tolerate racism? "Reality check: no race is better than any other in this mixed-up world." Neither will these young people participate in homophobia: "Love is blind—and blind to gender as well." And this generation's commitment to the environment is paramount. Andrew addresses a pointed letter to "Mother Earth," which is sobering: "We regret to inform you that we will no longer have any use for you. You have no more room for our trash, your air and water are polluted, and soon you will have no ozone. . . ."

Given the obvious power behind many of these declarations, the tenderness and innocence of this generation could be easily missed. Who can forget Miranda's letter to her best friend, Ashley Marie? Miranda remembers how they played together—coloring with a ninety-six-pack of crayons—from the age of four until Ashley Marie died in eighth grade. Miranda is writing her memories down as a present to Ashley Marie so that she "can take this letter to heaven" with her. She asks Ashley Marie, "What's it like up there in heaven without me?" And then there's Meredith, who writes to her deceased father that she dreads the future without his presence: "Who will hand your 'little peanut' over to the waiting groom . . . and who will be the grandfather to my children?"

Many letters we received are about loss—loss of innocence, loss of family through divorce or death, loss of trust through unreasonable and unhealthy societal demands. But a sense of hope shines through in even more of these letters—and not merely hope, but a commitment from teens to live responsibly and to improve our imperfect world. Samara identifies some of teen's "real worries" —that is, alcohol and drug abuse, breathing polluted air, and escalating violence. Crystal Lynn expands her thoughts, noting that "cheating, stealing, and killing are a part of everyday life."

In spite of these challenges, what we as the editors find absolutely amazing is their collective determination. Chris, for instance, galvanizes his peers in his letter and states that teens must simply "make an effort so we're not destined to repeat our history." And his refusal to blame other generations is generous, to say the least. Chris's final rallying cry speaks volumes about the prescient maturity of our young people: "Generation Y, what's happening around us is our fault, plain and simple. Let's just learn to face it—and start erasing it."

WHY WE DID THIS

This generation, which some call Generation Y, has inherited a distinctive legacy. They've also acquired some colorful labels including "the salad bowl generation," "Echo Boomers," "00 teens," "the Internet generation," "the Millennial Generation" and, simply, "Generation M." However they're described and whatever words they use to describe themselves, statistically speaking, the group is comprised of those born from 1979 to 1994. Seventy-eight million strong, they are one of the biggest population waves in U.S. history, more than three times the size of Generation X and rivaling the Baby Boomers. On the one hand, they live in the most globally connected and technologically advanced age ever. And, emerging as the largest age group in the United States since the baby boomers a half century ago, this generation seems more sophisticated than many adults remember themselves being at their age. But the unceasing barrage of violence, sex, drugs, and potentially lethal diseases that young people today must maneuver through is overwhelming and unprecedented. Bryan wearily expresses his generation's reality as this: "Daily life is a real struggle."

And it is. Consider Jonesboro, Arkansas, and Littleton, Colorado. These are only two sites where extreme violence was perpetrated by American teenagers. These horrific events leave us with troubling visions of young people so alienated from society—from basic standards of human decency—that we are left to wonder, stunned, "What went wrong?" With these violent events came a disturbing trend: in the effort to comprehend the incomprehensible, the general public seemed to categorize the young as a "tribe apart," as an antisocial breed that could not be understood. Newspapers bore boldfaced headlines screaming, "Kids Who Kill," while television producers aired specials on "The Lost Generation." Throughout, we repeatedly witnessed "experts" and "authorities" pontificating about the pressures teens faced. And yet we noticed that while reporters depicted teen behavior sensationally, few sources bothered to ask teens themselves for an accurate portrayal of their own lives. We were dismayed at how this ever-widening gulf of misunderstanding between teens and adults was being highlighted, even glamorized. To combat this us-versus-them mentality, we realized that a coming together was needed—an intergenerational bridge building.

In the aftermath of Littleton, Colorado, and the media barrage that followed, we decided to create a platform for young people to speak out about their lives in their own words and voices. We aren't psychologists who "study" teenagers or so-called experts or authorities on adolescents. We are two adults who are absolutely committed to hearing the teen experience from teens themselves. And what we heard most often, in one form or the other, was Tirzah's question, "What can I do to make a difference and help the world?"

As adults, we often mistake the public or portrayed side of teens as the only side; we forget about the private and secret self, which is masked. If young people have the courage to open their hearts, we as adults need to listen carefully, being sure to look beyond the exterior self.

Tragedies such as Littleton teach us that adults desperately need teens to communicate with us and educate us—about their anxieties and fears, their hopes and fantasies. Without this knowledge, we will continue to see them as lost. And they will continue to see us—adults—as strangers, when what they badly need are mentors, teachers, parents, and role models to believe in. It is our fervent hope that this book will serve as a springboard—a safe place for the teen and the adult to give and take, listen and receive, and, one day soon, to connect.

In 1936 Franklin Delano Roosevelt observed, "To some generations much is given. Of other generations, much is expected." We suspect that this is one generation to whom much is given—and from whom much is expected. Our goal as the editors of this book is to ask the individuals of this generation to explain, in their own words, the contradictions, realities, and, ultimately, the triumph of their lives.

About the Book

The call for letters began as a small endeavor. From the beginning, we knew that this was not a scientific, sociological study, with rigid tests and controls for validity. Instead, it was a labor of love, an example of what happens when good intentions and brave teens come together. We asked teachers to tell their students about our project; we haunted poetry readings given by high schoolers; we put the word out on-line.

Over the course of a year, this small, grassroots affair snowballed into a truly amazing movement. Friends were telling friends. Parents were calling teachers. School counselors were speaking to principals. And cousins in California were e-mailing relatives in Montana. Given the opportunity to put their own truths out there, young people roared back with an incredible response. Nearly five thousand letters came to us, all written by young people ranging from ages eleven to twenty—from Ohio to Ontario, North Carolina to New York.

And what did we ask teens to write about? Anything that mattered to them—their feelings about their parents' divorce, their experiences with drugs and alcohol, even their relationship with God. We asked them to write letters about anything that was important to them as young people—an issue or a grievance or a triumph that only the teen heart could articulate. We asked them if they wanted to address their letter to a younger sibling, telling their brother or sister something they wish they had known earlier, or to a teacher, letting educators know how lessons had positively or negatively affected their lives, or to a deceased family member or friend who was missed terribly.

All of these letters, and perhaps all of the adolescent experience, can be distilled into the push and pull of two opposing fields—innocence and experience. These contributions, while reflecting a diversity of adolescents in terms of class, ethnicity, religion, sexual orientation, geography, and race, share important similarities: they are reflective, poignant, and inspirational. And the letters will surprise you. You might expect to read a letter from the "jock" or the "druggie" or the "brain," because that's how adults often categorize young people. What we learned is that teens choose not to identify themselves that way. To them, more important than labels like "captain of the football team" or "class valedictorian" are the universal, emotional ties that bind.

We've divided the letters and excerpts into five headings: (1) What Adults Think Versus What Teens Know; (2) Influences; (3) Passages; (4) Challenges; and (5) Families. The letters in "What Adults Think Versus What Teens Know" introduce the reader to the secret heart of teens. In this section, young people share anxieties and hopes with the elder generation and with their peers. The letters in "Influences" touch upon key elements in a young person's life. In these intimate portraits, they ask themselves: How am I perceived? What makes me who I am? Factors like friendship and love, religion and race, come under the collective gaze of the contributors. In "Passages," young people learn life lessons when coping with the finality of death, sex, and divorce. "Challenges" illustrate the daily assault of substance abuse, harassment, and violence in the life of the young.

And finally, in the "Families" section, the letter writers address specific family members, such as parents, stepparents, grandparents, and siblings.

The significance of letter writers and their addressees cannot be overstated. Certainly no literary form is more revelatory, intimate, or individualistic. Dorothy Wordsworth once observed in a letter to her brother, William, that letters enable us to witness "the beauty of the inmost heart on paper." As this generation sets its course, it has absorbed some invaluable insights along the way—lessons not just for teens but for all of us. What our young people know, feel, and believe is grounded in their own experience. The first step to understanding this generation occurs when they—and we—place value upon their personal stories, their inmost hearts.

PART ONE

What Adults Think Versus What Teens Know

"We persevere in a world that doesn't want us. We will strive and rise like the Phoenix out of the fire with more knowledge and experience than any other generation in history."

—JAIME CASTAÑER–WEISS, AGE 14,
CAROLINA, PUERTO RICO

PART ONE

Declarations

Messages to the Elder Generation

WHAT ADULTS THINK

WHAT TEENS KNOW

Who I Am and Who I'll Be

TO TEENS FROM TEENS

WHAT ADULTS THINK VERSUS WHAT TEENS KNOW

LOOKING AHEAD

Doing Our Part

Declarations

America, We Move Forward

JULIA McBEE

Age 17, New York, New York

America, what happened to your face?
Where are those rosy cheeks
that perfect smile?
Your bright white teeth,
glaring at me, mocking my existence.
Where is that multicultural bullshit?
Looking at you, I am ill.
Everything you strived for
is lost.
That diversity,
those family values.
Just say no!
Spend some quality time with the 'rents.
Go to college.
Keep up those A's.

Talk it out, don't be afraid to be yourself.
What's wrong with you people?
Where have all of your trite values gone?
Mr. President, where's your return to family values?
America, the facade that you have been living behind
is ruined.
That picture-perfect world that you tried to create
is crumbling under my feet.
The bubble protecting your sheltered minds is popping.
I see through you and so does everybody else.
Nothing has changed.
We are told to speak out,
become an individual.

But your perfect mold has not melted yet.
It still attacks me.
The wax haunts me, it holds me down
conforming me
still.
I have to go to college.
Where's my free choice?
That's right, I have none.
But what am I complaining about?
I live a comfortable life,
I have everything at the tips of my fingers
and want to throw it all away.
How spoiled can I get?
Algeria is dying
and all I can do is complain about what I don't have.
I don't have real problems
like starvation, like sickness, like poverty.
I must dwell on the vexing details of my life to pass the time.
Where's my prescription to ease the pain?

All this corruption is a part of life.
It makes sense.
If it didn't happen
life wouldn't be the same.
This chaos comforts me.
All these problems make up our society.
Where would we be without them?
Nowhere, that's where.
We know this, so we don't solve our problems.
But they have a limiting factor.
Soon they will encompass the spectrum.
We'll get there anyway.
If solved, if left alone
we move forward.
JULIA MCBEE

Looking, Searching, Yearning

VIVIAN IP

Age 17, Englewood Cliffs, New Jersey

Dear America,

I am looking for leaders. I am looking for the mothers and fathers who do more than think they understand the new generation, which is stuffed with twenty-four-hour AOL and flashy MTV videos. I am looking for the psychiatrists who know the real feeling of loneliness on a Saturday night, wandering around a dead town that can only offer pot and a naked romp on an empty football field. I am searching for the elders who can tell me whether or not they've really left anything for me to live for.

What does my generation do when we have Kurt Cobain as a poster boy, a suicidal druggie who couldn't understand life but lived long enough to express his frustration? Dear America, you have lived past the rock 'n' roll craze of the fifties, the activism of the sixties, the flower power of the seventies, and the heroin addicts of the eighties. But now you have created teenagers who thrive on drugs and bitterness. We are what you could call a mindless talk show, a nonsolving run-on sentence filled with mistakes and misplaced words. As your obese dysfunctional families sit home with potato chips and watch fake lives on TV, teenagers everywhere are the lost effect of every cause. We are, in simple terms, lost.

America, I'm bored. I'm so bored, I feel useless because the struggle for control is slipping through the cracks in the sidewalk. You, America, who pretends racism is going away with those new TV programs and a multicultural variety of kids. You, America, who let a nation of people point embarrassing fingers at a president who is trying to Band-Aid the world. And what did you let our society leaders do but lie straight to our faces, claiming butter-coated words as "the truth"? Besides, who knows who our society's leaders are anymore? Go ask someone on the street. Princess Di and the Spice Girls? Funny, I thought they were British. Who would have known that the media has such an impact on our lives? The problem starts with staying alive amid the loneliness and misunderstanding that technology has blessed and damned us with. The problem starts with the white noise America the Beautiful has been buried under. The problem starts with the future and what we have lost from the past.

Back before telephones were necessary and the Internet was vital, children used to talk to their neighbors, skip around the park, and "go outside and play." The definition of that last phrase used to be that we kids would run around outside for hours on end, coming home right after dark, dirty and happy to a mother waiting to yell about germs. Back then, fun physical exercise wasn't priced at $299.99 and delivered by UPS in a long cardboard box stamped with "30-day money-back guarantee." Back then, I would have remembered silence.

But now it's the nineties, and it's noise, noise, noise. People are screaming from windows. America, please silence yourself! Our lives are defined by running circles around one another. Newspapers are filled with trash talk about divorce, murder, suicide, and the latest fashion or health craze. My generation stands at our public toilet bowl, flushing morals and ethics down like thin toilet paper. The constant buzz that's stuck in my ear is slowly weakening my belief that you, America, were about the love of freedom. Don't get me wrong. I love freedom, you love freedom, Americans love freedom—but not when freedom comes in a Pandora's box that slowly lights more dynamite with every decade.

And maybe that's what I'm really looking for: peace and quiet. Maybe already at my young age, I have abandoned the thought of having leaders to solve anything, and what I really need is the respect of hearing someone say "excuse me" on a busy street or "How can I help you?" in an adult store.

I jadedly attend my school with the passing of student faces and bodies like rats stuck in a hole. I stiffly sit in my classroom, learning about the past that has made and shaped you, America, the greatest country in the world. I numbly blind myself because of the noise that has devoured my presence in this land where everyone is screaming. I am numb. I am numb, and so is every old young person I know. To think I was ever innocent—what a joke.

I am seventeen, America, and I want a cause, a movement, a war. I want a leader. I want unity and respect. I am young and I have the right to freedom. I have the right to scream my head off every single day of the week. I have the right to dial the 1-800 number and shout at the operator, telling them their product sucks and never did work. I have the right to tell anyone and everyone to fuck off whenever I feel like it, but, dear America, after seventeen years, what I really yearn for is silence. Do I have a right to that, too?

Hopefully,

VIVIAN IP

"The "grown-ups" of the world today point a lot of fingers at us. They say our generation will be the end of the future, but if you look at it long enough, we're not running the world yet, and it still is going to hell!"

—ANGELA KAPPES, AGE 13, FLAGSTAFF, ARIZONA

"Some kids have given the rest of us a *bad* reputation, and I think that is not fair."

—STÉFANNY BEAUDOIN, AGE 13,
CRESTON, BRITISH COLUMBIA, CANADA

"Just because we have our own style and we talk in a "different" language, does that mean that we're up to no good?! Listen, if any 'elders' are reading this, get a clue, we're not you! Think about that."

—STEVE ST. PIERRE, AGE 14,
KANATA, ONTARIO, CANADA

Messages to the Elder Generation

WHAT ADULTS THINK

Why Do You Think Teens Are So Evil?

BRYAN SIMONSON

Age 15, Pocatello, Idaho

Dear People:

Why do you think teens are so evil? It's not like every single teen is a bad person. Most of us are just struggling through high school and trying to have fun at the same time.

It's probably quite difficult for you to understand since you've long since stepped out of our shoes and found a new, better-looking pair. But not all teens are sex–crazed–evil–doing maniacs.

Generally, we're just a busy group of young people involved with our peers, our families, school, sports, and we participate in a lot of activities besides playing shooting or drug games. What I want you all to understand is that daily life is a real struggle. That you hold it against us is very annoying, to say the least.

I'll tell you what, though. If I ever find out that teens *have* really become the nightmares you assume we are, I'll tell. I promise. But I guarantee that I will have gotten a new pair of shoes by then.

BRYAN SIMONSON

"After the tragedy at Columbine, adults see us as the Devil."

—Audra Adam, age 15, Hampton, Virginia

"You don't know how hard it is to be a teenager these days. So many things like gangs and drugs, and then those anorexic models out there make you feel like you're not good enough. . . ."

—Sherri Holen, age 13, Clovis, California

"As a child, my parents and teachers always told me that I could be anything that I wanted to be. Yet as a teenager, I just hear what kind of things everyone else wants me to be."

—Valerie Seimas, age 17, Tracy, California

Just Because I'm a Teenager Doesn't Mean That I'm Like Every Teen You Know

STEFFANIE WILDE

Age 14, Cedar Springs, Michigan

Dear Adults of the World,

I am fourteen years old. I may be less than half your age or maybe even a third! You might have kids or even grandchildren my age. *Just because I am younger doesn't mean that I don't have a voice.* I deserve respect, and I have as much right to be listened to as someone twice my age.

You're listening now, aren't you? I've caught your attention because I have an attitude and because I'm a teenager. Everyone wants to know what goes on in the head of a teenager. But I am an individual. I'm not like every other or, for that matter, *any* other teenager who walks this planet. *Just because I am a teenager doesn't mean I am like every other teen you know.*

The reason you need to get inside our heads is because you'd like to understand us. You're giving it your best shot, and you *don't* know what it's like. Times have changed, and we have different experiences, different goals, and different lives from those you had. *Just because you were a teenager doesn't mean you understand.* In other words, even if you were once the same age as me, it doesn't necessarily make us similar. You were and are different from me; I am and will be different from you—but maybe we can try to get along.

With best regards,

STEFFANIE

WHAT TEENS KNOW

"High school has taught me many lessons, but I've been thinking about lost innocence lately—innocence lost at parties, through drinking, dating, and sometimes even drugs."

—TIFFANY PENDOLA, AGE 14, BUFFALO, NEW YORK

"Drugs can do harmful things to our bodies and we try to learn this, but does it do any good if you put actors and actresses snorting cocaine up their noses on TV?"

—APRIL HOLLE, AGE 16, CONCORDIA, KANSAS

The End Often Justifies the Means

MATT MACKEY

Age 15, Granite Bay, California

Dear Educators,

My letter is in regard to what I feel has become an epidemic in high schools across the country. At my high school, the pressure to receive good grades is almost unbearable. Nowadays, it is not good enough to get just decent grades or even good grades. To get into a good college, and remain competitive, you must earn a grade point average often in excess of a 4.0. This can be done by taking honors and advanced classes such as AP courses. This pressure often causes students to take nearly impossible schedules, which leaves students with a never-ending barrage of homework. This makes a social life nearly impossible! Also, it takes away from what I believe to be a good high school experience.

Now onto my main point. Because of the tremendous pressures put on students to do well in school, students often resort to a technique all of us at one time or another have resorted to, a technique that both educators and students are familiar with: cheating!

While cheating may be wrong, in a student's eyes it may be the only way to do well on what seems like an impossible assignment. As the pressure to do well increases and the stakes grow higher, a sense of urgency and the decision to take a greater risk also increase. For many students such as me, the end often justifies the means.

Sincerely,
MATT MACKEY

“ Dear Mr. President:

Upon recent discussion with many of my peers, we, the Children of America, have concluded that your conduct was unbecoming of an American president. Listen, Mr. President, we know what you are capable of. And don't feel that everyone pities you because of what happened, because you know what? We don't pity you at all. You brought it all on yourself. Now be a man and take the blame."

—GINA DENJEN, AGE 13, BERWICK, PENNSYLVANIA

"I don't judge people by their appearance, just how they treat me. Just try to find out what people are like inside and have the courage to befriend them in spite of their history or their outward appearance. I believe that this process allows us to truly be who we are and that it enables us all to be understood and to understand."

—JACQUELINE LICHT, AGE 16, WILSON, NEW YORK

Dear Mother Earth, We Will Mourn Your Loss

ANDREW DAVID WEBB HUSTON

Age 16, Cincinnati, Ohio

Dear Mother Earth,

We regret to inform you that we will no longer have any use for you.

You have no more room for our trash, your air and water are polluted, and soon you will have no ozone; the sun will surely burn us alive when it is gone. Termination of your job is to take effect as of now. You have twenty-four hours to pick up what natural resources you have left in your desk before we head for space to destroy yet another planet. Your service here over the years has been top-notch, and we would be glad to write you a recommendation for new employment despite your current uselessness.

We will mourn your loss. But remember, it is better to burn out than fade away, and you're sure to combust in a wild conflagration when our rocket boosters soar back down to ignite our wastes. All in all, it was nice visiting with you, but we wouldn't want to live here.

Maybe God will help you; after all, he/she did claim to create you. Ashes to ashes, dust to dust, we raped you. If you want to sue, tough shit. Justice doesn't apply to you. Your check is in the mail, but it will probably bounce!

Sincerely,

THE YOUNG PEOPLE OF THE WORLD

To the Elder Generation, Look to Us

SAMARA SHEVER RIPPS

Age 16, New York, New York

To Americans over the age of 21:

I'm sick and tired of hearing horror stories about teenagers on the evening news. They're all about "killer kids" or the rising rate of juvenile delinquency. . . .

I'm regularly followed around in stores, where I watch adults assess me and find me guilty of being a teenager. Of course, they assume I'll try to shoplift. I'm even stopped on the train on my way home and asked why I'm not in school—this is after I've just spent a full day in classes.

You know, it's really a bit ironic. I see ads on television or in magazines about people wanting to feel as carefree as "the young." But I'm not carefree. I have worries—real worries—and they have nothing to do with the fact that I don't have a boyfriend or that there might be alcohol or drugs available at a party I go to. Those are simply facts.

What do I worry about? I worry what will happen to the kids at the residential center where I volunteer when they are aged-out. I worry what will happen to our wildlife if we continue abusing our environment and natural surroundings. I worry that I'll have no control over whether my children will have clean air to breathe. I worry about cancer and AIDS and gun control—and not because I smoke or sleep around or think someone I know intends to shoot me. The point is, in today's world, how can I not worry?

I'm convinced that my generation has been given a bad name because of a few isolated and crazy young people. But I need you to understand that we're not a generation of damaged people. Rather, we're a large, talented, and diverse generation. We're more tolerant of one another than our parents' generation is. And the Internet, which is seen as some sort of dangerous tool in our hands, is one reason why we have the distinction of being the most globally connected generation yet.

Instead of fearing us, you in the elder generation should look to us for inspiration because we still have the energy and the dreams that you have long ago forgotten. Maybe I'm naive—something few in my generation claim to be—but I still believe that one person can change the world, and I plan to give it my best shot.

SAMARA SHEVER RIPPS

Who I Am and Who I'll Be

TO TEENS FROM TEENS

People Look at Me and See a Pierced Eyebrow and a Bad Attitude

KEVIN E. HAIGHT

Age 18, Salisbury, North Carolina

Hello. Bonjour. Hola. Aloha. Howdy. Hallo. Bonjourno.

I've got a problem . . . the thing is, I didn't start it, but I'm willing to help end it. What's my problem? The narrow-minded world I live in . . . that *we* live in.

Most of us are guilty of stereotyping, making assumptions about people based solely on their appearance, and we do it because it makes life easier for us somehow. When you meet me, you might only see a pierced eyebrow and a bad attitude, and you might not stop to talk to me because it's easier to turn away or walk off and stare. But don't be afraid or stare at me—come right up and talk to me—you'll be quite surprised, I promise.

We all look at each other and automatically make assumptions, and even though I'm writing about it, I'm guilty of it at times. But at least I can admit I'm doing it. When we see an obese person having trouble walking, we don't even think twice about making fun of them. But have you ever stopped to help them or find out what kind of person they are? Have you ever sat down and talked with a "freak" that has piercings, tatoos, and spiked hair?

If you aren't narrow-minded, you might find that they're quite interesting and even have a purpose behind the way they dress or act . . .

Sincerely,

Kevin E. Haight

Generation Y, Face It—And Start Erasing It

CHRIS PAGE

Age 16, Paris, Tennessee

To my fellow teens:

We've experienced a multitude of crimes by people of our own age recently, and the depressing thing is that the hate crimes and the murders are still happening. You know, what's frightening is the ease with which we all recall these incidents. Remember the gruesome shootings at Columbine High School in Colorado? Then there was the racist incident involving the black man who was mutilated by being dragged behind a pickup truck. And how could we ever forget the tragic shootings in Paducah, Kentucky?—one of the first places to fall victim to the kind of tragedy we're all used to now.

If you think about it, you'll see that the individuals who committed these crimes shared one important thing: each and every one of them blamed society for having driven him to commit these unspeakable acts.

Sometimes I wonder: are we so different from these teens in the sense that we won't accept responsibility, either? Think about it. What's really sick about all of this is the fact that we, as one nation and one world, refuse to accept blame for what we've become. Instead, we're too busy blaming television, movies, music, or video games. Surely these things have some negative influences, but are they, in themselves, really what make teens act in such unconscionable ways? Of course not!

We need to realize that we're destroying our own species—and jeopardizing future generations—by blaming these other influences. I think we can start by believing that the solution for this social problem is within all of us. Why not start by doing simple things like communicating with our parents a little more? After all, they were our age at one time, too, and have valuable insights. Guys, the point is that we really have to make an effort so we're not destined to repeat our history.

Generation Y, what's happening around us is our fault, plain and simple. Let's just learn to face it—and start erasing it.

CHRIS PAGE

> "In every storm there's a rainbow and in every person a heart. Don't be afraid to use your heart. It will get you to a lot of good places."
>
> —AIMÉE BECKER, AGE 16, OAKVILLE, MISSOURI

> "Know that you're special. And do *not* shake your head when you read this like I know you will. You really are. And when you realize it, you'll be mad at yourself for not figuring it out sooner."
>
> —BRIANA BROWN, AGE 15, BAYFIELD, ONTARIO, CANADA

LOOKING AHEAD

You May Not Have Heard My Name, but Someday You Will

CHRISTINE QUON

Age 13, Culver City, California

Dear World,

You may not have heard my name anywhere or seen my face, but someday you will. Someday I will be that incredible girl in every magazine, on every television screen, and on every person's mind.

Do not be afraid of me because I will be a role model—a hero, an idol. I will exude a healthy sense of self-esteem and have a lively image and beauty as well, although I recognize that beauty is not always seen.

These are all the things I wish for, but a wise teen knows that when you wish for something, to give up on it is not to wish at all. I will not give up. I will persevere until I reach the moon, and, if possible, I won't stop there. . . .

So, remember my name, and I'll remember my directions, and someday, somehow, some way, I will be your Queen.

CHRISTINE QUON

“ Many teens want to be gymnasts or movie stars or have other glamorous, money-making jobs. Me, I think

I'll choose the road less taken. To write, and to put words on paper that somehow make a story. That's what is best for me.”

—KELSEY RUBENKING, AGE 11, LAKEWOOD, OHIO

“Crime makes the streets dangerous;
Parents hush my speech.
I feel no adventures will come my way if I stay at home.
My real life won't start until I'm on my own.”

—TIRZAH O'BEIRNE, AGE 17, WINDHAM, MAINE

Give Us Light in Our Lives, and Let Us Give That Light to Others

STACEY PLANCER

Age 15, Rancho Cordova, California

Dear World,

We are teenagers, and with that comes certain responsibilities. You do not understand us, and because of that, you fear us. You see us as things to be watched—abusers of drugs and alcohol, slaughterers of our fellow schoolmates. But not all of us are like that, World. You have to see the truth inside us. Perhaps if, instead of fearing us, you really noticed us for who we are, these bad things that you see would stop happening.

World, eventually the future will become the past, and the children of today will become the leaders of tomorrow. We will be presidents, senators, mayors, and some of you will be gone. You have to understand that and know that there is nothing you can do to stop it. We will be great men and women, World, but not if you don't help us. We need you to talk to us, not as if you are older and understand more, not as if you know what we are going through in our hectic lives, but as if you are equals to us.

All that we ask of you, World, is that you give us a chance. We can be all that you want us to be and more. Give us light in our lives, and let us give that light to others. We can do anything you want us to do, anything we believe we can do. Give us a chance. We're not all bad, World.

Just help us out a little. We'll handle the rest.

STACEY PLANCER

Dear Me, in the Year 2012

RAINE McLEOD

Age 17, Cayley, Alberta, Canada

Dear Me—Raine:

I guess it is the year 2012, if you are reading this. Hmm, I wonder how things are. As I sit here typing a letter to myself, I am in Cayley, a town you've probably forgotten. Remember all the fun times you had in Grand Cache before you had to leave?

I keep thinking about the look on my face in thirteen years, when I find my own letter full of hopefully inspirational things and little tidbits of information that will most likely be necessary in later life. This may sound cheesy.

So, onward . . .

- Remember your goals. Do whatever it takes to do what you want with your life.
- Tell Mum and Dah that you love them. They love you. You know they do.
- Live in New York at least once. And don't be afraid of the traffic there. Just follow the signs (and the guy in front of you).
- Be a singer or a masseuse. After all, those are the only things that you are really good at. At least, that's how it is now.
- No problem can't be solved with a little confrontation.
- Don't be afraid to tell the truth.
- Don't kill things unless they are suffering. Simply capture and relocate them.
- Don't be afraid of spiders. They can't hurt you, and the ones that can don't live here; they're in Brazil and Arizona.
- Nothing is worth killing yourself over. Not even love. Come to think of it, not even hate.
- Don't jump to conclusions, and don't assume things.
- Things aren't always as they seem. People have to earn your trust.
- Don't let yourself be used. You aren't a pawn.
- If you have a kid, love it. Don't lie to it. Tell it everything it wants to know. Even awkward things, like what an orgasm is.

- Don't regret stuff.
- Love and be loved. Live and let live.
- When someone hurts you, tell them. Don't hide. You are completely entitled to your emotions.
- Remember Wiccan law: "And it harm none, do as thou wilt." Smart, huh?
- Things will happen as they well should. Maybe not as you planned, but, hey, nothing ever will.
- Discover new things. Worry not about what will happen or what has happened, but what *is* happening. Hell, don't even worry. There's probably nothing you can do, and it causes gray hairs.
- Depend on yourself. That way, if you let yourself down, there's no one else to blame.
- As you talk to people about what you think, keep one thing in mind. They are allowed to different opinions than you. Everyone is entitled. *Everyone*. No one is wrong, and you are not always right.
- Don't *not* change because you are afraid people will notice. They might, and deep down inside, that's what you want, isn't it? You want people to see and hear you.
- Don't be afraid to like someone nobody else does. Maybe other people don't get him.
- Lose weight only for yourself.
- Try hard at everything you do. Try not to go half-assed on anything.
- Be a good person. Be tactful but truthful, honest but polite. It will pay off. When people know that you won't lie about them, they'll value your opinion more.
- Watch sappy movies. A good cry now and then is soul food.

- You are variable. You can change your mind whenever you want. Have reasons to back up your opinion, though.

There. I think that's all. Have a nice life.
—Me

Doing Our Part

Love Your Neighbor

KARI PHELAN
Age 15, Barneveld, Wisconsin

To Whom It May Concern:

Gun violence, teen violence—you know what I'm talking about. Who do we blame? Why did it happen? First of all, let's consider how invested we are in finding scapegoats—in finding someone or something to blame.

Face it, there's nobody to blame but ourselves. Think back to elementary school—back to that quiet kid who never spoke, sat in the corner, and didn't interact with anyone. She or he probably didn't have many friends, if any. Ten years later, we hear that this same person set off a bomb at school and killed the history teacher. Could one reason be because they had so much anger and loneliness inside and nobody tried to help?

And who and what do we blame? The Internet, maybe, or musicians and negative lyrics or maybe celebrities and violent movies—basically anybody but ourselves because the guilt would be too much. Maybe we should stop creating outcasts. Maybe we should realize that when you get down to it, we aren't so different. And maybe the next time someone walks past you with what you consider a weird haircut or strange mannerism, you'll stop and think: this person might become my best friend.

The biblical saying "Love your neighbor" epitomizes everything I'm saying. And if we love our neighbor, it might just save us.

KARI PHELAN

A Smile of Appreciation

GENNA CAJIO

Age 15, Edgewater Park, New Jersey

To anybody who will listen:

I understand that so many people go through life without noticing the world around them. My question is, why? Why would you not look at, and appreciate, the beauty that constantly surrounds us?

To not notice an ocean full of life or a new flower with tremendous potential is a shame. Some people are even oblivious to the virtues that other people possess. Sorry for the cliché, but everybody *is* beautiful in their own way. And not to recognize that is wrong.

Why not stop and smile in appreciation of beauty and virtue? Everybody looks their best when they smile with innocence and purity and appreciation.

A child, for instance, knows how to appreciate, to live life. Because I have a desire to become an elementary school teacher, I've watched a lot of children. And they are definitely an inspiration to me because of their no-nonsense personalities and the liveliness they possess. They know when to smell a rose and smile. Children know how to cheer someone up and to encourage others just by seeing beauty around them.

As we get older, we forget to notice the dewdrops on a rose petal, descending into the tiny world beneath. We forget to notice a couple sitting quietly on a park bench as their little ones play on the swing set. We are blind to the happiness and love of a group of friends just having fun together.

It is a damn shame that we often recognize our appreciation only when it is too late to share it with others. Why can't we just open our eyes and be like children again? Children are the strongest beings because they are not afraid to acknowledge their feelings of love to anyone.

So, when the world seems to be passing you by, "stop and smell the roses." Also, remember to tell others of your appreciation by smiling!

All the best,

GENNA CAJIO

"I'm not perfect—I've made mistakes but have always taken full responsibility for my actions, and I have dealt with the consequences. I just wish there were more teenagers in this world that would do the same."

—KERA MORTON, AGE 17, ANADARKO, OKLAHOMA

Tell Those You Take for Granted How Much You Love Them

KELSIE LAINE GERLACH

Age 16, Castle Rock, Colorado

My grandmother was recently diagnosed with cancer. She has already had three different types of cancer, and while she's a robust woman, I wonder if she'll pull through this time. Her body is getting so tired.

You know, no one thinks that this kind of loss happens in their family, and I once thought the same way. But look at me now. I've already lost my favorite aunt to cancer, and I am about to lose my precious Nana to it as well. Still, I try not to obsess about the cancer that's ravaging her but focus instead on the wonderful moments we've shared.

Please, do something for me: before you sleep tonight, think about all those people you might take for granted. And tomorrow, surprise them by letting them know how much you love them. Believe me, it makes all the difference.

KELSIE LAINE GERLACH

"Why can't the world slow down? Why can't we stop and notice the people around us for a change? Other people who are starving for a warm smile, a little attention, and love."

—LAURA FRYE, AGE 17, AIDA, OKLAHOMA

Dear World, You Deserve More Respect Than You Normally Receive

THEA WINGERT

Age 15, Red Deer, Alberta, Canada

Dear World,

You deserve more respect than you normally receive.

You bring life, shelter, and a sense of belonging to all creatures who are born upon your beautiful soil. You let the sun burn your loving skin, the wind whip at your face, and you even let us tear you apart just so we can live in comfort. It's true that every once in a while you lose your temper and cause a tornado or an earthquake. You're entitled to it.

I, as a human, promise to continue to take care of you. I will plant more trees, pick up my garbage, and walk to school. I will educate those who are naïve to your generosity, and I will not give up until you are as bright and shining as the first day you offered yourself to us humans.

THEA

> “The world. What an interesting, magical, scary, loving, hungry, and wonderful place it is.”
>
> —TARA LLOYD, AGE 15, TORONTO, ONTARIO, CANADA

PART TWO

Influences

"Think about a standard test. One of the questions is about your race/ethnicity, and it gives you choices: African-American, Native-American, Asian, Caucasian, Latino, or Other.

From now on, put "Other" and pencil in "Human.""

—KEVIN E. HAIGHT, AGE 18,
SALISBURY, NORTH CAROLINA

PART TWO

Friendship

HOW FRIENDSHIP HELPS

HOW FRIENDSHIP HINDERS

The Heart

THE CRUSH

LOVE FOUND

LOVE LOST

INFLUENCES

Religion

Race

Teachers

Friendship

HOW FRIENDSHIP HELPS

Not Ahead or Behind, but Side by Side

JULIE KATE KENWORTHY

Age 15, Little Rock, Arkansas

John,

Do you know that you are my best friend?

Unlike some best friends, we didn't grow up together. We can't read each other's minds. We haven't even known each other all that long. But in the short time that I've known you, you are always the person I can turn to when I need a friend.

We invented our own little language that only the two of us can understand, and when others stare at us like we're crazy, we just look back at them the same way. You helped me break out of an abusive relationship by proving that my ex-boyfriend was a jerk who was taking advantage of me. You showed me many times that suicide wasn't the answer.

I showed you how much you really care for your girlfriend. I taught you why cheating on her isn't right and how it can only end in pain. I taught you to love yourself for who you really are and that you don't need to wear a mask, since you are already special.

Do you know that you are my best friend? Thanks for always sticking by me. You never take a step ahead of me or fall behind me. We are side by side.

I love you,

JULIE

There's Always a Spot at The Dinner Table for You

VALERIE OLSON

Age 14, Merrimack, New Hampshire

Dear Big Brother,

I've always looked up to you in awe. Though there are five years between us, and although we weren't always the closest, you were—and are still—a big part of my life.

When I found out you were doing drugs, I wasn't sure how to react. I don't totally disapprove—it's your life and your decision, after all. But sometimes I worry that you might be getting into drugs that might seriously hurt you. I wasn't able to talk to you about how I felt before, although I wish I had before you moved.

So, now you're gone. Right before you left, I overheard mom saying that you "had to come back and eat dinner with us at least once a week or your sister would be very upset!" It's the truth, though I knew she said it because she worries about you, too.

Please stay safe wherever you go, Kevin. Know that the couch is always ready if you need a place to sleep, and there's always a spot at the dinner table with a hot plate of food. And if you're ever in any trouble, we're here no matter what. Don't forget we care.

Love, your little sister,
VALERIE

"You're a part of me. . . . You know how much I love you, and even though we never say it, it has to be said. I want to take this chance to tell you that you will always be the one person with free access to my heart. Guys will come and guys will go, but friends will stay forever. I trust you with my life. . . . I'd go to the ends of the earth and back for you. All I ask of you is that you believe that."

—KARYN FRICK, AGE 17,
TOM PRICE, AUSTRALIA

HOW FRIENDSHIP HINDERS

I Refuse to Be Your Fool

TORI ROSIN

Age 20, Ames, Iowa

To the Person I Used to Call Friend:

You don't know when to stop, do you?

When I was younger, dumber, or just more desperate for attention, you made it seem like I was lucky to have you around. According to you, your friendship would save me from the abyss that was our school and from the darkness that resided inside my mind.

And I was grateful for your hand, extended to save me from drowning. Perhaps for too long.

The unexpected happened though—I wised up. The hands came off my eyes, and I started to see how you truly acted. Why were my looks and actions constantly watched and ripped apart and recapped for all to share, when you were clearly not the ideal, either? Why were my emotions and instincts constantly ignored, mocked, or interrupted, when yours had to be analyzed immediately? Why was I pushed into situations I didn't want to be in? If we were anywhere that made you uncomfortable, I never prolonged your suffering.

If this is how you treat your friends, I am afraid of how you leave your enemies. It's taken me too long, but I've realized I am not a freak. Sometimes I even like who I am—no thanks to you.

So why do you keep on coming back to me? I don't think I'm the last sucker to have walked the earth.

No matter what, I refuse to be your fool.

Sincerely,

TORI

I Was a Sheep

MARICAR BAQUIR

Age 14, British Columbia, Canada

To Nichol,

Nichol, we used to be the best of friends, at least I thought so. Now, looking back, I realize that I was a sheep. I listened to your every word, tried to act like you, and agreed with almost everything you said. In short, I thought you were my heroine. But I see now how wrong I was.

I'm not saying you are a bad person, but I am saying that you made me popular and I liked it, so I did everything I could to stay friends with you. One of those things was changing myself.

I was once a thoughtful and shy girl, afraid of others. But you made me see that being outgoing was "in"—so I tried it. Everyone seemed to like that side better, so I acted like a fake, ignored the real me, and became what everyone wanted. I became what I thought *you* wanted. This was because I felt that I owed you for making me popular and because I thought that being friends with you brought me closer to the "in" crowd. Yes, in a way, I used you. Shamelessly.

When we came to high school, everything dissolved—our friendship, my devotion to you, my popularity. I suppose in losing a friend and a rank, I gained a piece of myself. But that doesn't mean it didn't hurt.

Nichol, I know that you probably won't end up reading this, but in a way, writing this helps me to be true to myself.

MARICAR

"There are people in this world who are going to hurt you, some purposefully, some accidentally, and some who won't even realize they did it. They may make you start to doubt yourself or others, but if anything, you should start to doubt *them*."

—COURTNEY MCCREADY, AGE 16, MERCER ISLAND, WASHINGTON

The Heart

THE CRUSH

Dear Cupid, Save a Special Arrow for Me

JENNI NORMAN

Age 16, Albemarle, North Carolina

Dear Cupid,

Sixteen is too young to feel so old. I think that love must truly be blind because in all of my sixteen years, it's done nothing but stumble past me, groping someone else. I'm beginning to feel like a comic old spinster, waiting for love to come knocking while I have to witness my friends fall. . . .

There was a time, though, when I did believe I was in love. I carried on this struggling relationship in my imagination while the object of my affection remained oblivious. I might have crashed hard, but if there's one thing I garnered from that infatuation, it was a great poetic muse. My journal is filled with wistful poetry. In a way, I guess I was like a little child who couldn't understand why she shouldn't touch a hot stove again after burning her hand. But eventually I learned.

Sometimes—well, all right, most of the time—I can't understand why your arrow has bypassed me. But I do believe that my attributes are many and that it will just take someone special to appreciate them. This, I know, will take time.

Cupid, I know you're saving a special arrow for me. Shoot at your will.

Sincerely,

Jenni Norman

Crush and Crushed

JESSIE CHARDOULIAS

Age 16, Glenwood, Iowa

About my ex-crush:

I have had many crushes in my measly fifteen years but have been hurt only once, and I will remember it for the rest of my life. I was a freshman, and I thought James was the most adorable, sweetest, smartest, and all-around perfect guy. And the greatest thing was that he seemed to like me, too, which was a miracle in itself. I mean, to think that James, a senior no less, actually liked little old me was a truly magnificent thought.

Homecoming came around, and James never asked me to be his date. So I went to the dance reluctantly but was having fun dancing with my friends. Then, suddenly, I was in heaven. My obsession actually wanted to be near me: James had asked me to dance. And by dancing, I do mean slow dancing—up close and personal. It was amazing.

From then on, James was the only man for me.

I thought about James all the time—in science class, study hall, lunch, while going to the bathroom—you know, *all* the time. My friends concluded that I had completely lost it. Every topic led me back to thoughts of James. Maybe it was how attractive he looked in his wrestling outfit (specifically, in his red sweatpants), or it could be the color of his eyes or anything else that made him seem like a god.

I dreamed about James and even named our children! Okay, this is something I'm not entirely proud of, but I was smitten—what can I say? James was my first serious crush. I attended every basketball game because I knew he'd be there. We would get into skittle and paper fights, which I realize is childish, but I always took it as a positive sign that he actually liked me.

But as the school year progressed, he wasn't as nice. All of a sudden, I was being shoved into lockers, constantly teased, and having shoes thrown at my head. Friends of mine told me to forget James—that he was inconsiderate and simply not good for me. According to them, all he ever did was "mess with girls' minds and hearts." I refused to believe them.

One night, at a basketball game of course, I learned that everything my friends had told me was absolutely true. My stubbornness and lack of experience had caused me to get a broken heart; it took me six months to figure out that James was a jerk. One minute he was winking and blowing kisses at me, and then when I showed interest, he just snatched up my heart and smashed it! That fast! The entire thing took all of ten minutes. I can still remember James walking away with a grin on his face, looking all arrogant.

James took a piece of my heart that night as well as the innocence of my childhood. Although I knew it had to happen sooner or later, I suppose I was really hoping it would happen later. Still, the experience forced me to step out into the real world and to let go of a certain childish naïveté. While I didn't want to believe it at the time, James proved to me that people aren't always what they seem. Also, I learned that friends can provide important insights, and sometimes the hardest things to hear from them can be the most helpful.

Although my memories of James aren't entirely positive, the

skittle fights, his hugs, and those whispered "I love yous" (even though they weren't sincere) will always be dear to my heart. Don't worry, I'm not in denial. I fully realize that James was just a crush. Still, he was *my* crush—my James, and I learned some invaluable lessons as a result of this experience. Perhaps the best thing is that it has taught me to fight for what I want, for what I believe in. And for that, James, I thank you!

JESSIE CHARDOULIAS

LOVE FOUND

Waiting

JESSICA HEIKKILA

Age 17, Lamoni, Iowa

Dear Benjamin,

You're my best friend in the world, but there are still some things I'm not sure you'll ever understand.

When we were younger and first became friends, I liked you immensely. I mean, it meant so much that you, a high schooler, paid attention to me, a middle schooler. I wanted to be in your world, and before I knew it I was.

Suddenly, you wanted to date me, and instead of being truthful, I lied to you. I said that I just didn't like you "that way." The first three months after I told you this were very hard, do you remember?

But then, one day you called me, just like you used to, and we were friends again. You guided me through high school, showing me the ropes, hanging out with me, even helping me get my first boyfriend. And when I realized that the chemistry wasn't there with him, you helped me survive the breakup.

All of a sudden, things changed drastically. I found myself flirting with you and was astonished when you flirted back. When you asked me if I wanted to pursue our relationship, I was floating on air. Imagine, I was barely a junior, and already so many wonderful things were happening!

Maybe that's why I was so devastated when my friend, Charity, died. I knew you wanted me to run to you for comfort, but I honestly thought I could handle it on my own—and you know how I'm embarrassed to cry. I didn't even realize it at the time, but I was in a deep depression over Christmas; I never wanted to go anywhere, felt like I had no friends, blamed myself for Charity's death. And even when I finally accepted the fact that she was gone, I felt such intense anxiety in public. Maybe I thought everyone blamed me. All I know is that I couldn't do anything without literally shaking. I couldn't pursue all those life-affirming things I'd always loved—playing my clarinet, singing, dancing. I guess what ultimately happened is that I lost all hope and faith in myself.

It was so difficult then, and for a while we were even going to break up. I was convinced it would help, remember? But you told me to take some time out for myself instead of being with you every moment. That hurt at first, but then, slowly, I began realizing how right you were. I began rediscovering myself, and after two months of depression, I experienced a complete turnaround.

I'm now to the point where I can actually see the road I took; I know now that I was in guidance the entire time. You never let me give up, even when I felt isolated and thought no one cared. You helped me in so many ways, Benjamin. I honestly can't imagine my life without you, without the friends we share, without the joyous times we've had, and even without the painful times we've endured.

All I'm left to say, Benjamin, is this: I love you—and I am beyond grateful.

JESSICA

He's All That

LIZ THERIEN

Age 17, Havelock, Ontario, Canada

My dearest sister,

The most wonderful thing has happened to me. I'm in love.

And it's not one of those physical things. It's real, true love. Tim is sweet and charming and tender. He knows exactly what he wants out of life, and he still manages to be gentle and understanding. He won't do anything if he knows or thinks it will hurt me. We have so much in common, and yet I've learned so much from him, as he has from me. I believe he might just be the "one." No, I know he is.

He gives me peace of mind. He makes everything bad seem so unimportant. He'll wrap his arms around me, and everything will be perfect, like I'm in heaven. When his lips meet mine, it's like every kiss I've ever received from others had been merely fragments of what a kiss really is. He makes me melt.

He inspires me. I've written so much since I've met him. And we've become the best of friends. I go to him about everything. He knows my deepest secrets, my greatest fears and desires, my hopes and dreams. He shares those dreams.

I couldn't imagine my life without him. I see us growing old together, having children. We've even talked about getting married. Can you believe it? At our age! At first I thought it was crazy—we're only seventeen. But it feels right; just talking about it makes every day seem worth living.

The other day we were sitting on the couch holding each other, just talking about anything, and it dawned on me that everything is going to be all right. What a weird thought, but it was there. And it's the truest thought I've had in so long. With him in my life, whether it be as a friend or more, everything's gonna be all right.

Well, I guess all I have written sounds silly to you, since you're so much older and still think yourself too young to fall in love. I can tell you now that when you find the one, you will know.

Until next time, sweet sister,

Liz

> "Love feels the way chocolate tastes—bitter at times, but almost always sweet. That is how real love feels."
>
> —Jill Anderson, age 17, Salmon, Idaho

LOVE LOST

The Burden of Pain a Hero Must Bear

DONNY CUMMINGS

Age 17, Washington, DC

This topic concerns every single person in the world: True Love.

This fatal subject has caused much pain and much happiness. No wars can compare to the suffering one suffers when one is denied it, and no utopia can compare to the bliss one feels when one experiences it. Whether we are weak or strong, whether we are emotional cripples or we try desperately to convince ourselves that we are not prey to these feelings, love gets to all of us in one way or another.

I'm a teen who has prided himself on clear thinking and self-honesty. Still, there is one thing that I—and probably many of us—lie to ourselves about. If you've ever fallen for someone—really fallen—then you'll know what I'm talking about.

Think about that special person. That individual whom you would gladly suffer a million injustices just to be able to hold for a fleeting instant. And then you lose this person, and in order to cope with the grief you tell yourself that the feeling will surely fade in time or that you were never really in love in the first place. But the evasions don't work, and the truth lurks. It wallows in the back of your mind, ready to strike you down when you're at your weakest.

I should know. I have recently taken the plunge and would instantly accept any suffering you would throw at me just to be with her. The problem is that she has a boyfriend and they're in love. What complicates matters is that she's also my best friend. So you see, there's no escaping her presence—I can't even rejuvenate my weakened spirit for a short time.

Believe me, I've tried to suppress my feelings. I almost did it successfully, too. What crushed it was that one night I overheard her and her boyfriend making love; I heard her moan with the pleasure that I so desperately yearned to give her. It honestly felt like my heart was being crushed from within. And there was absolutely nothing I could do.

The very next day, would you believe that she and her boyfriend had a fight? And I mean an all-out warfare kind of fight. It was one of those situations in which a relationship can be destroyed forever.

Since I am her best friend, she came to me for support and guidance. You can imagine how intensely I wanted to blow up the issue so that I might have a chance at happiness with her. But when I looked into her eyes, I was helpless; all I could do was to explain things from her boyfriend's viewpoint. I tried my hardest to defend his behavior so that she could understand it—and forgive him. Then I went to her boyfriend and did the same thing.

Am I a fool? I sit here and wonder, did I do the right thing? My friend says that this is the burden of pain a hero must bear. I guess it was the noble thing to do. Whatever you want to call it, it was just the thing that had to be done.

I believe that no one has a right to ruin or jeopardize someone else's chance for happiness just so they might have a shot at their own. Still, the pain is there in me—and it's still growing.

Is this simply the burden of growing up? What would you have done?

Donny Cummings

My Future Without You

STEPHANIE LEVASSEUR

Age 17, Baudette, Minnesota

My Tony,

Two days ago, I had no way of knowing we'd break up because of "what's best" for me. *I* don't even know what's best for me, so it's a damn good thing you do! I guess I'm glad someone is looking out for me.

It's really hard to believe that college is close enough to become a reality and close enough to affect my life—and affect us. College always seemed so far off in the future. And now it really scares me, thinking about it and realizing that everything I do in this one moment has the capability of affecting my future.

All this future talk. What is the future, anyway? And the big question—what is my future without you?

I started to realize that maybe things weren't going to work out just as I had imagined and dreamed that they would. And yet I wished that we could live happily ever after. I didn't know how, but I hoped we'd stay together during college. Other couples do it, and I figured our love was so strong that we could handle anything and college would just be a simple obstacle easily overcome.

After college, I didn't know what would happen. We'd be married, of course, maybe with kids. By then you'd know what you wanted to do and I'd be working my way up the *New York Times* best-seller list. Whatever our future was, I figured as long as we were together, we'd do fine.

Remember last spring when you threatened to kidnap me, saying you couldn't wait any longer to be with me? You drove and drove—out past the movie theater, both of us crying, and the radio softly playing, "Do you wanna get married, or run away?" It fit the moment. We held on to each other and cried and promised that we'd get through it all and be together.

Maybe there's a chance that after college and "through it all," we'll be okay, and we'll fall back into place with each other where it just feels right. But if college and futures and career and life take you away from me forever, at least I'll never forget you and all the memories we share.

And we can try to be simple friends now, and we can try to make it easier on both of us when I leave to begin my future without you, but this heart aches for you now and for all the future that I can imagine.

"If you love something, set it free. If it comes back to you, it is yours. If it doesn't, it never was."

All my love,

STEPHANIE

Love Crept Up on Me in the Form of a 5'6", Blond, Virginia Beach Beauty

RYAN BLISS

Age 20, McLean, Virginia

Dear Tricia,

I want to express to you the way that I feel, and since we haven't spoken in so long, writing to you seems to be the only solution. I don't know if I will ever see you again or even hear the sound of your voice. But I hope that you will read this and maybe understand the way I feel.

Apologizing now for the horrible things I said to you that warm, spring day so long ago may not change any feelings you have toward me, but I cannot live with myself any longer if I do not at least try.

When we met, we were fifteen years old, freshmen at a Catholic high school. Who would think that we would eventually fall in love, talking of marriage, looking into the future, planning our lives together?

Even at the height of our relationship, I do not think you ever understood what you meant to me. You were my first, and I have never respected, idolized, or loved anyone as I did and still do you. To you I was just another boyfriend, but to me, you were perfection, all that I could ever want, all that I was made for.

Some men and women strive to fulfill the nagging, painful urge for love all their lives. And I found it so soon! Love just crept up on me in the form of a 5'6", blond, Virginia Beach beauty.

But where did we go wrong?

Was it something I said? Something I did? You said you had changed. And I don't understand. We were only apart for three weeks. How does three weeks apart change someone after months of never leaving each other's sides?

When you left, I didn't know what to do. My best friend, my teacher, my guide, my lover—you were all of those to me, and then you were gone. I had nowhere to turn, nowhere to run. You sent me out into the night with no hand to hold, no light to pierce the infinite darkness.

How long has it been since we've been apart, a year and four months? I'm surprised I can't tell you the exact number of days. I still see your face, and I still hear your voice. And I'm sorry if it was me who drove you away because I miss you. And if I had one wish, one lucky penny, or even just one last chance, I would go back to that day and simply say, I love you.

RYAN

Religion

HOW RELIGION HEALS

The Heart of Love

RAY SMITH

Age 14, Mount Marion, New York

My name is Ray Smith, and I'm fourteen years old. In fourteen years, I've come to one conclusion: the only way I can get through each day is to have the Lord in my heart.

I'd like to share a story with you, a special story illustrating how God has helped me.

I was born with an abnormal heart. The first five years of my life were spent running back and forth to doctors and hospitals for tests, X rays, catheterizations, and three open-heart surgeries.

I'll never forget the long days in the hospital. My mom was always by my side and stayed in my room. We found many ways to pass the time—playing checkers, telling stories, watching the show *Alf* on television—and I always looked forward to my dad visiting me on his days off from work. He'd bring my younger sister, Heather, who was two or three at the time, and she always did antics to make me laugh. I guess this is one reason why she and I have grown up to be so close.

My last surgery happened when I turned five; I actually spent my birthday in the hospital. However, despite the surgeries, I had an atrial flutter, which means that my heart would beat two hundred times a minute—and this could last for hours. When this happened, I was terrified. But I found solace in my family; we would pray together, acknowledging that God was in control of my life. Unfortunately, the atrial flutter grew worse, and finally my parents decided to home-school Heather and me. In some ways, this made things easier, but my health only worsened.

On November 7, 1997, after a sleepless night, I was taken to my cardiologist's office. I was experiencing heart failure and was rushed to one hospital, then to another. I just felt so tired.

I can still remember being surrounded by a team of doctors and nurses and getting pricked with needles over and over. It was at that moment that I prayed what was undoubtedly the hardest prayer of my life. I prayed to God that the pain was so overwhelming that if it was time for me to go to heaven, to please let me go, and if it wasn't my time yet, to please make the pain end. My mother was standing close to me holding my hand, and I told her that I loved her. I remember looking at her face and seeing her glow with a beautiful light. Three hours later I woke up. I was told that they had tried to convert my heart rate four times with no success. There was still discussion of surgery, but my cardiologist, Dr. Reda Shaher, who had taken care of me for fourteen years, corrected the atrial flutter by changing my medicine.

Two weeks later, I experienced a different heartache when I received a call saying that Dr. Shaher had passed away from a massive heart attack. This was a heartache that human medicine couldn't touch. He had become more than my doctor; he had become my friend. Again, it was through God that I found peace.

My life continued. A month later, I met Joe Torre at a Starlight Children's Foundation event. Joe was incredibly kind and even invited me to the Yankee dugout. It was the thrill of my life! I wasn't able to play competitive ball because of my heart condition, and here I was sitting with some of the best ballplayers and coaches that ever lived. I even became friends with one of the players who is also a Christian. We agreed that Christ was the highlight of our lives.

In July I threw out the opening pitch in our hometown Babe Ruth tournament. This summer I was asked to keep score for the Babe Ruth League. I am a Junior Red Cap for our American Heart Association chapter this year and was the leader for the "Friends and Family" group. I've also been busy making radio announcements and have been participating in raising money for the upcoming heart walk. I feel like God is helping me to help others—to give to people.

As I turn fifteen years old in three days, I want to lean even more on God—to try always to please him. I don't know what my life holds, but I know if God was with me these last fourteen years, that he'll never desert me now. I have also learned that the physical condition of the heart is important, but it's what's in the heart that counts.

My advice to anyone who's afraid or worried is to trust in God. No matter what happens, my friends, God always promises to be there for you.

RAY SMITH

Dear God, I Never Thanked You for Sending Down Your Angels to Save Me

MELYNDA M. ALLEN

Age 16, Milford, Illinois

Dear God,

I just wanted to say thank you. There was that time when you helped me with the problems I was having with my parents. You helped me realize that they really loved me.

There was also the time when I didn't have many friends. You taught me to make new ones and rekindle the old.

God, you always helped me to feel better about myself when I felt ugly or stupid. I always knew because of you that I was special. I never thanked you for loving me, either. I always knew that there was someone who loved me.

Remember when I lost control of my car and almost wrecked? I never thanked you for sending down your angels to save me.

Oh, and God, there's one other thing I'd like to thank you for. Thank you for sending your son to die on the cross for me. *Thank you.*

Love,
Your Daughter,
MELYNDA

HOW RELIGION HURTS

God, Where Are You?

MIKE KWIATKOWSKI

Age 17, Hamilton Square, New Jersey

Dear God,

Our world is dying. We need your help. All people care about anymore is themselves. And the people who want to live the correct, proper way have no idea where to turn for help. Everybody claims they know you, even though they all say something completely different about who you are or what you want. Either that or they just flat out claim you don't exist.

There are so many religions in the world, each saying it is correct in its beliefs, each with its own set of legitimate miracles. Consequently, followers of one particular belief think that the others are wrong and shun the people who hold those beliefs. Humanity then becomes divided in their worship of you. Is this what you wanted?

We need you. We can't solve our problems. People throw their newborns in the trash or go into school and shoot their classmates. Why do you allow this to happen? It is said that you love us. We need your guidance, and we need it now. Faith isn't working anymore. It's so hard to believe in a being who loves everyone when people are hurting, raping, and killing one another. How can you love the rapist, the murderers? And why do you not love the victims enough to save them from that agony?

Countless hours are spent in prayer to you. Requests, demands, questions. I just want to know the right thing to do, the right way to live. That's all. I would happily place myself in your hands and do whatever it is you want me to do. But I ask you, and I get silence. I ask people, but everyone has a different answer. They all claim they're right. Faith simply isn't enough. So I just have one question to ask of you.

Where are you?

MIKE

"Society has the power to change things. Years ago, when someone took another's life or raped or did something terribly wrong, they were put to death. People today get off in a few years for everything, it seems like. How about life in prison? Or death if you rape or murder someone? Have we lost sight of what is important now? Is being harder on crime the answer? I turn to God, as many do, with one question: *why?* I try to have the utmost faith in God, but how could he watch his children hurt so badly?"

—SARAH LLOYD, AGE 19, TRAFFORD, PENNSYLVANIA

"God:

I just wanted you to know that down here, in this place we call earth, there is a girl who still believes in you, but I'm also very confused."

—ISADORA VELÁZQUEZ, AGE 15, MIAMI, FLORIDA

Reaping What We Sow

CHAD HOOPER

Age 15, Selden, New York

To Those Without the Answers:

I think it started when they complained that they didn't want any prayer in our schools. We said okay.

Then someone said, "You better not read the Bible in school, the Bible that says, 'Thou shalt not kill,' 'Thou shalt not steal,' and 'Love your neighbor as yourself.'" And we said okay.

Remember Dr. Benjamin Spock, who said we shouldn't spank our children when they misbehave, because their little personalities would be warped and we might damage their self-esteem? We said okay to that, too.

Then someone said that teachers and principals better not discipline students. Our administrators said, "Whoa, no teachers in this school better touch a student when they misbehave, because we don't want any bad publicity, and we surely don't want to be sued." We said okay.

Then someone else said, "Let's give our sons and daughters all the condoms they want, so they can have all the 'fun' they desire, and we won't have to tell their parents." And we said okay.

Then someone said, "Let our daughters have abortions if they want, and we won't have to tell their parents." We said okay to that, too.

Then some of our top officials said that it doesn't matter what we do in private, as long as we do our jobs. We said, "As long as I have a job and the economy is good, it doesn't matter to me what anyone does in private. It's nobody's business." In short, we said that it's okay.

So, now we're asking ourselves why some of our children have no conscience, no concept of consequences, why our children don't know right from wrong, and why it doesn't bother them to kill. Probably, if we think about it long and hard enough, we can figure it out.

I think it has a great deal to do with "we reap what we sow."

Okay?

Signed,

CHAD HOOPER

Race

RACISM

African-American Men Have a Heavy Load to Pull

MARSHALA LEE

Age 14, Greenwood, Mississippi

African-American men have a heavy load to pull.

We're automatically categorized by society as being sports stars, high school dropouts, jailbirds, drug dealers, or drug addicts. We're constantly under surveillance like some foreign animal. America does not like to see African-Americans, especially men, succeed in life.

America needs to open its eyes and realize that we want to—and will—be heard. We have willpower and won't stop until we have achieved equal status.

MARSHALA LEE

Everyone Assumes That Because I'm Black, All I Listen to Is Rap

TAUHEEDA YASIN

Age 17, Vienna, Virginia

I'm tired of being so aware of my race all the time.

It seems like every day in school, I'm aware of my skin and how different I am from everyone else. In the middle of class discussions, when we're talking about black people, I feel everyone get on edge and turn to look at me, wondering if I'll get offended.

I try to be understanding, but it gets fatiguing when everyone assumes that because I'm black, all I listen to is rap music. Or that because I'm black, if my hair is long, then it has to be fake. Or that because I'm black, I talk Ebonics.

TAUHEEDA YASIN

"I write to you as someone with hope. Hope that we will live in a world where your difference does not mean you are an outcast or hated, so that if you are black or white or Asian or Hispanic, it just won't matter."

—BRITTNEY NEIDHARDT, AGE 17, SAUKVILLE, WISCONSIN

"Being twelve, and having one black parent and one white parent, it would seem sort of silly for me to be racist against anyone really."

—LEMUEL H. THORNTON III, AGE 12,
PATRICK AIR FORCE BASE, FLORIDA

"Some people are black. Some are white. Some are brown, and some are mixed. People can't see that everyone is made perfectly.

What does it matter if everyone's skin color isn't exactly the same? Aren't we the same on the inside? Don't we all have hearts, brains, and, most important, feelings?"

—BRITTANY SHEARER, AGE 12, AMBRIDGE, PENNSYLVANIA

"Reality check: no race is better than any other in this mixed-up world."

—JENNIFER KIVISTO, AGE 14,
THUNDER BAY, ONTARIO, CANADA

"Categorizing is a form of hatred. He's black, she's white. Get past all that and look at the person themselves. Not their shell; rather, their soul. We could do some very great things as a unit, working together to become a race that's together and whole.

Just think what we could accomplish then."

—JOSH GUENTHNER, AGE 16, IMPERIAL, CALIFORNIA

"My father didn't approve of me dating any race apart from white. When I began dating a man from Mexico, my family simply didn't know what to make of me. But I don't mind. At least I know who I am."

—JANUARY MORLEY, AGE 18,
NEW HOPE, KENTUCKY

Teachers

HOW TEACHERS BETRAY

Dear Sir, Your Legacy Is Guilt and Shame

ELEANOR CLIFT

Age 18, Wangaratta, Victoria, Australia

Dear Sir,

Perhaps it was wrong for me to even use *dear* in this situation, since you're anything but. . . .

You are the man who violated my trust. You are the man who stole my innocence. You are the teacher who destroyed my faith in others. Your legacy is guilt and shame and nightmares that I can't wake up from.

While you get promotions, I run from you in the corridor. That's unfair. Maybe that's the one thing I can thank you for, teaching me that life is never fair. One day I might have the courage to tell you face-to-face what I think of you, but for now I'll suffer in silence and pray that one day you'll realize what you did.

Thank you for nothing.

ELEANOR CLIFT

"Mr. Cordle,

Before you go putting limits on women, think about how you would feel if you had limits put on you."

—MELODY LITTLE, AGE 13, AMANDA, OHIO

"Whenever I get skipped over, and a boy is asked to help a little piece of me cries. In my opinion, we are all equal. In our hearts and in our minds."

—SABRINA JANSMA, AGE 16, NORFOLK, NEBRASKA

"I'm tired of teachers who don't want to teach. I'm tired of teachers who don't really want to be teachers and, in fact, hate kids, period. Some teachers are about control. Some teachers like the fact that they can control how young people think, and that is a problem."

—TAUHEEDA YASIN, AGE 17, VIENNA, VIRGINIA

HOW TEACHERS INSPIRE

You Have Made Me a Better Person

ALIZABETH BERG

Age 13, Ronan, Montana

To the world's teachers—

It's the teachers I would like to thank in this letter—and one teacher in particular.

My teacher is an amazingly talented, intelligent, caring person. He repeatedly claims that he has rarely been told that he's improved a person's life, but I know better! Perhaps they just didn't know quite how to say it. There were many times that I wished I had found the words to tell him, but I didn't.

So, here it is. Mr. Quaile, I want you to know, one way or another, that you have made me a better person. Your priorities, morals, and values . . . have taught me that there are decent people out there and that I don't have to be a certain way because that is what is expected. I know, because of you, that I can set my own standards and that I can say no to the things I am certain are wrong.

Maybe I'll have a great career when I get older, or maybe I'll stay at home and raise a family. But you taught me that if I choose to be the best I can, it is all I need . . . and that God is smiling at the way I live my life. For the record, Mr. Quaile, now at least one person has told you how she feels. Thank you for always letting your students know that you teach because you care about us. You make a difference, whether you are told or not.

God Bless,

ALIZABETH BERG

From the Corner to College

RAQUEL McLELLAN

Age 17, Los Angeles, California

Dear Mama Holt,

I know that sometimes in class I didn't always seem appreciative of you, but I was and I still am. You've touched so many lives through your teaching, and you've made a special impact on mine.

When I arrived in your classroom three years ago, I didn't believe in myself or much else, for that matter. You believed in me, and as a consequence of your faith, I learned to believe in myself. You've dedicated your life to helping kids, and I can feel how proud you are of everyone who has ever passed through your door. You pushed me to succeed when my inclination was to sit silent in the corner.

Mama Holt, your official title might be "teacher," but you've extended yourself way beyond that. You're a true friend, a comedian, a believer, a mentor, and a mother to all your students.

RAQUEL MCLELLAN

P.S. Without your help, I never would have applied to college. Can you believe I'll be a college freshman this fall?

PART THREE

Passages

"In loss, we finally realize that nothing lasts forever, that happiness is finite, and that no one is immortal."

—IRWAN KURNIAWAN MUHAMMAD, AGE 19,
PAHANG DARUL MARMUR, MALAYSIA

PART THREE

Sexuality

ON VIRGINITY

GETTING PHYSICAL

GAY/LESBIAN

ON MOTHERHOOD

Divorce

PASSAGES

Death

Sex

ON VIRGINITY

Guys, Look into My Soul Instead of into My Shirt

KARA-KAYE COLLEY

Age 16, Jamaica, Wisconsin

Boys:

Let me be clear. I developed early, started wearing a bra at eight years old, and wore a size D cup by the time I was thirteen. I don't mind you admiring my full-figured body. No, that's actually quite flattering. What I do mind is the way some of you have tried to get inside my pants.

It would be a wonderful change to be appreciated for my mind, to have guys talk to my face instead of to my breasts, to have a guy look into my soul instead of into my shirt. . . .

So, for now, I opt for my legs remaining locked. I wear my imaginary chastity belt with pride. I have nothing to prove to any guy, and if he doesn't like it, he can kiss my black posterior.

I will adorn myself with the armor of God with the hopes that he will shield me from yielding to temptation. I shall recall the countless lectures—the ones my mother thought I wasn't listening to—and will always carry with me the honor, pride, and respect of my family. These things give me all the strength I need in the battle to maintain my virginity.

KARA

Virgins . . .

CRYSTAL LYNN CARR

Age 16, Monticello, Mississippi

Virgins

Are

Becoming

Obsolete.

"Maybe I'm just different. I don't take drugs, drink, or smoke. To tell you the truth, I've never even wanted to. I have a boyfriend and am totally in love but refuse to have sex. I believe that it should be saved for your wedding night. . . .

I figure, why ruin my body, mind, and future?"

—JACQUELINE LICHT, AGE 16, WILSON, NEW YORK

" Sometimes I feel like a major freak being a seventeen-year-old virgin. . . .

At times I suspect that my life would simply be easier if I were to just get it over with one time when I am drunk. It's like a disease, virginity. People look at you different when they hear that you're a virgin. "

—MARY WIEDE, AGE 17, BYRON, TEXAS

GETTING PHYSICAL

I'm Not the Chicken of a Girl You Think I Am

AALEEYA UMEDALY SPENCE

Age 16, Corvallis, Oregon

Mother, in this letter I will say exactly how I feel and show you who I really am. I'm your daughter, but I am simply not the little girl you thought you still had. I'm not the chicken of a girl that you think I am, nor am I the angel that I claim to be.

I love you more than life—more than anything imaginable. You've always been the pillar of our family's strength. When Dad died, I wanted to kill myself, but I lived for you. You're the reason that I'm still here to walk the earth. I've always looked up to you as the ideal person. Oh, Mom, I'm sorry.

When I met Alex, it was amazing. The electricity, the connection, the perfect match. We hit it off immediately but were careful to take it slowly. Then, suddenly, it became love. Mom, almost overnight I was in love. I couldn't believe it; I was scared of what that meant. I knew what people did when they are in love, but sex was scary for me, and you would never approve.

But it happened. After five and a half months of being together, we did it. I made love to him, and it was wonderful—magical even. But I was ashamed to think how you might react to it and what you might do. That's why every time you tried to ask, I replied, "Mom, come on. I'm a chicken, remember?"

Except that I'm not. And this is the first thing in all my life that I haven't told you. Mom, I don't want to hurt or disappoint you in any way. And I'm sorry if I have.

You have been my idol and the pillar of strength in my life—and I want to keep it that way. You've always been proud of me and my achievements, and I'm frightened of how this could jeopardize that.

Don't judge harshly, Mother. I'm still the same girl I was yesterday. I love you.

AALEEYA

GAY/LESBIAN

Love Is Blind—and Blind to Gender as Well

ALEXIS STARK

Age 15, Roswell, New Mexico

To the Future,

The most prominent issue in my life is sexuality. I'm gay. Yeah, call me a dyke, throw insults at me, I don't really care. The truth is, you don't understand. You don't know who I am, and you don't know what it means to be me.

You can't tell me I made this decision, and you can't tell me that God hates me. I'm not listening to that anymore. I'm done with the guilt, and I'm done with the questioning. Please. End your hatred, and end this suffering. Love is love, be it friendship, familial love, true love, or puppy love. And love between two humans is simply that—person to person. It has been said that love is blind, and it is blind to gender as well.

So open your minds and your hearts. End the hatred, the violence, the suicide, and the misinformation. Do you realize that 30 percent of suicides among adolescents are by teenagers who are queer? This is deeply upsetting, not to mention disproportionate, considering that only 10 percent of the population is gay or lesbian.

Ignorance is not bliss, and hatred is nothing to be admired. We are all human. Rejoice in our similarities, and rejoice in our differences. Let no more tragedies like Matthew Shepard's take place.

The Bible says, "Love casteth out fear." Don't be afraid of me.

The Bible says, "Love thy neighbor." I'm here, this is our planet; love me.

ALEXIS

"Everyone should be allowed to experience love and making love on their terms. Gay and lesbian people should not be shamed, spat upon, or cursed."

—TEGHAN MERCER, AGE 14,
BUNDABERG, QUEENSLAND, AUSTRALIA

"I am sick and tired of you people who discriminate against gay, bisexual, and lesbian people. *What are you so intimidated by?*"

—LEANNE HUNTLEY, AGE 13, WILLASTON, SOUTH AUSTRALIA

ON MOTHERHOOD

My Link with Mothers Everywhere

MELODY NICHOL

Age 19, Hastings, New Zealand

To the World:

When I was eighteen, I had the most precious gift anyone could give me—my son. I don't know what I would have done if I'd lost him because he's now my world, my life, my link with mothers everywhere.

MELODY

Divorce

Happiness Does Not Always Mean Togetherness

MAUREEN TRACY TAÑEDO
Age 14, Metro Manila, Philippines

Dearest Mom and Dad,

My life will never be complete without both of you. After all, you are the reason I'm alive today and I am who I am. I'm proud to say that despite all the trials we have undergone, I'm a happy young woman. My happiness is something I will forever cherish; it's something that will forever remain in my heart. Happiness is special; it cannot be bought, and it does not always mean togetherness.

Life has never been a bed of roses for us. I know you know that. The annulment of your marriage was rough and tough for not just you but me as well. I was only seven years old, and I thought that my life had ended right then and there. I still remember the deafening scream that echoed through my mind throughout the annulment. I was wrong, of course, but I thought that there was no more reason to live. I guess it's because there seemed to be a hidden rule of belonging to a "perfect family" when I was younger. As I grew older, however, I gradually understood that your decision was for the better.

I'm grateful for one thing regarding the annulment, though. I used to swim in shallow waters, hoping only for material things to come my way. Through this incident, my eyes were opened to a world of reality—and closed to a naive world of perfection that I had tried to make my life match.

I've remained silent about my feelings about the annulment for years. I chose not to be vocal about this for fear that opening up would destroy my perfect world and would equal rejection. Now, with hope, I open up and pray that my healing will last a lifetime.

I understand and have forgiven, yet I have not forgotten. Nothing happens in this world by chance; this I have accepted fully. It has taken me this long—over seven years—to fully forgive myself and everyone involved, but it was definitely worth the wait. For now, I am happy with who and what I am. I cannot ask for anything more because I know both of you respect me for who I am.

Do you both realize just how much I love you? I may not say this often, but you are the roots of my life. You've held my soul during those times when I felt like I was falling into the abyss.

Mom and Dad, you inflame my life, and you complete me.

With love,

MAUREEN

"Mom and Dad,

I learned the most important thing from my childhood from the two of you. I learned that I want to act the way you two do toward everyone but each other.

I mean, you two could be anti–soul mates instead of soul mates. . . . It's baffling and incredibly sad, really. You show kindness, respect, and tolerance toward everyone *except* each other. . . ."

—RACHEL MUZIKA, AGE 15, DELMONT, PENNSYLVANIA

Dropping the Big D-Bomb

TOREA JADE SCHAUER

Age 15, Milwaukee, Oregon

Dearest, dearest father,

Finally. The perfect opportunity to confront you. And there is no way that you can walk away now. Yes, you must listen to and accept these brutal truths.

What went wrong? Between you and me; between you and Mom; between you and the rest of the world? I was always your precious, perfect little girl. Well, for ten years anyway. We would cook up crazy ideas, make up fun nicknames for each other, and wreak havoc upon our household. It was delightful. I loved you.

Then along came that one fateful day. I can still feel the tension and still remember the events as if it were yesterday. You had been distant all week. Mom took us to a science museum while you began to pack. And when we returned, you both dropped the big D-bomb on us: divorce. It's crazy, but I distinctly remember foraging through our cabinets to find you peanut butter, which, for some reason, I had come to the conclusion that you couldn't live without. And then you were gone.

And yes, even postapocalypse, there were some good times, I think. However, they are overshadowed by the general dismay I felt every time I was yanked away from you at the end of each gruesomely uncomfortable weekend visit. And I know it hurt you as well. Soon we began to drift apart. You were a bit unpolished and new to the bachelor scene; I was young and opinionated. Perhaps even judgmental. And I'm sorry.

However, Dad, that gives you absolutely no excuse to play the mind games that you played. My "Daddy-o rockin' on a patio" was essentially dead, and you took his place. There is no reason at all, other than the obstinacy on both our parts, why I haven't seen you for more than fifteen minutes at a time in the last four years.

And perhaps what hurts me the most, Father, is that you live only half an hour away. It's not as if I haven't made concerted efforts to include you in my life. I've kept track of it. There have been upwards of twenty missed concerts. Countless soccer games. All my cheerleading performances. All of which you were invited to, cordially, by me.

I know you'll regret this someday. Maybe not today. Maybe not tomorrow. Perhaps not until we are both very, very old, when I have finally forgiven you for not being in my life, supporting me and the rest of our family. And you'll finally realize it; the cloud of indifference that has been inhibiting you from seeing the real deal will be lifted, and you'll see that I'm a woman and you've missed the best times of both our lives.

So I'm sorry, Father, but eternally grateful. Your lack of presence has made me a stronger, more independent person. I can't say I'm not bitter. But I don't regret a moment of the life I've lived thus far.

Sincerely, your one and only daughter,

TORI-O

You Left Thirteen Years Ago Without a Good-bye or a Trace of a Kiss

MICHELLE LEA SAMPERTON

Age 15, Fredericksburg, Virginia

Dear Mother,

Even though you and Dad are divorced, you are always here with me helping me through all my bad times and guiding me day by day. I haven't seen you or even heard from you in thirteen years, but you'll always be in my heart. I want to tell you honestly about my life, even though you'll probably never read this letter unless some miracle happens.

I always look at the few pictures I have of you—such a beautiful woman—and wonder if I'm ever going to talk to you or touch your skin and tell you how much I have missed you. You made vows to be with my father 'til death do you part, but you took that promise away. You left without even saying good-bye and without a trace of a kiss.

Mom, that Sunday afternoon changed my life completely. You walked out on two precious children, children who didn't expect the unexpected. Year by year passed, and there was no trace of you. The family did everything possible to find you but to no avail. All I know of you now is your name and a few pictures. I don't even know your birthday; no one ever told me.

My father says that he doesn't understand why I want to find you since you deserted us in the first place. But all I know is that you're my mother and no one can change the way I feel about you.

I have a new stepmother now, and sometimes it's difficult because she has her own son and daughter. It hurts to see that they have a mother and I don't. Even though you're alive in my heart and memory, who will I talk to about my first crush? Who'll give me advice about dating? You won't even know when I get my first job or get married or pregnant.

I heard through the grapevine that you have three children now with another man. I hope you don't hurt them the way you've hurt me and my family.

Every year I have a special wish on the eve of my birthday: I pray that maybe for that birthday, you'll think of me and try to find me. I treasure that thought forever. Until we get in touch, though, I guess the closest I'll get to being with you is talking about you or praying for you in my heart.

Your daughter,

MICHELLE

Death

DEATH OF A FRIEND

What's It Like Up There in Heaven Without Me?

MIRANDA HART

Age 14, Bell Ewart, Ontario, Canada

Dear Ashley Marie Jenkins-Hill,

What's it like up there in heaven without me?

Do you remember how we played together when we were both four? We'd color with a ninety-six-pack of crayons and amuse ourselves for hours. Even when we headed off to kindergarten, we had identical notebooks, backpacks, and crayons.

During summers both our families vacationed in Florida. I remember how giddy the rides made us! And we'd share a bed.

Remember playing Marco Polo in the community pool? You could never find me, so I would take over for you because I was your best friend.

Then there was first grade. We were both in Ms. Kline's class. She had just finished college and was awfully nice—buying us treats and letting us have a party every last day of the month.

Second grade was also fun because we were together. Then the summer came and you got sick. I accompanied you to the hospital and doctor's office, and I remember the doctor said you had a cancer called leukemia. You stayed at the hospital all summer, and I visited you every day.

Third grade came around. You had no hair and were skinny, but the cancer was gone! Again, we shared everything from lunches to pencil crayons. Remember James, the class bully? I beat him up and made him cry because he always made fun of you.

Everything was fine, and summers came and went until the seventh grade. The cancer returned with a vengeance, and you got intensely sick. You were in the hospital so long that your parents eventually got you a tutor.

Then more tragedy struck: your father died in a car accident.

Grade eight began, and you were forced to wear a big, clunky machine. Kids teased you because you had cancer and were bald. Finally your mother pulled you out of school and home-schooled you after work. In the summer of that year, you were informed that you only had three months to live. I saw you as much as possible, and you died slowly—and in tremendous pain.

Ashley Marie, I am writing this letter to take to heaven with you. I miss you.

You were more than my best friend; you were my sister.

Miranda

DEATH OF FAMILY MEMBERS

Who Will Hand Your "Little Peanut" to the Waiting Groom?

MEREDITH ANNE HARRISON

Age 15, Marlton, New Jersey

Dad:

It's been seven long years now since you passed away. In those years, you've missed a lot—moments of fear, pain, love, joy, and moments where I've felt like my entire soul is crumbling. It's been so difficult without your guiding hand, your encouraging smile, and your loudest cheers. Oh, how I've yearned to feel your arms wrapped around me with an "I'm so proud of you, Meredith." But now I just rely on worn-out memories to get me by.

I haven't the faintest idea how different life might be if you were still here. Would I be the same person with the same friends, the same interests? Would I have experienced the same failures? Would I still have the same stand on certain issues? Would I have made the same mistakes? I guess now I will never know.

Sometimes at night I cry myself to sleep asking God why he took you away. Maybe he thought I would be able to handle it, but I still haven't decided whether or not I'm able to do that. For one thing, if you were still around, I wouldn't be constantly fighting with Mom. And maybe I wouldn't be so angry at the world if I could still hear your soothing words.

As if your absence isn't hard enough right now, I dread the future and all it holds without you. Who will hand your "little peanut" over to the waiting groom? I so desperately want it to be you. And who will be the grandfather to my children? They deserve nothing less than the best, which, in my eyes, can only ever be you. It's truly not fair that they should be deprived of ever meeting such an amazing man. But then again, when has this entire situation been fair?

My life has dramatically changed since you were taken away on that night long ago. I can't really say whether it was for the best or for the worst because I really just don't know. But the one thing I do know is this: you were my father, you are my father, you will always be my father, and my love for you can never be surpassed by anyone. I miss you dearly, and I hope to see you again in another life.

Love always,

MEREDITH—YOUR LITTLE PEANUT

How Could We Have Known It Was the Last Time We'd Ever Speak?

CHRIS MORGAN KAJIN

Age 16, Forsyth, Montana

Dear Nick,

So, how's it been? Can you believe it's been four years since we were last together? It seems like just yesterday when you said good-bye. How could we have known it was the last time we'd ever speak?

I'm growing up and trying to follow in your footsteps, but it's hard. And there's another thing, Nick, I'm not you. I have to make my own way if I ever want to make a real difference in this world and try to change it for the better.

You know that I've never been good with words, and writing this doesn't come easy. But I'm doing it anyway because I hope someday you'll read it and know that I still love you and think of you. . . .

Do you realize that you've taught me to live life to the fullest—and to go out and experience people and the world? It's true; you influenced me to learn, to live, and to love.

And I bet you didn't know that you're a legend at Takachsin? You did so much that people still look up to you after all this time. And Tewalt actually has "Remember Nick" written on the underside of his hat so that whenever he does something, he tries just a little harder so that you'd be proud.

Now Alicia is experiencing the same thing I did four years ago when you died. Her little sister was struck by lightning and killed instantly. How can I not understand intimately what Alicia's going through? The truth is that you can never fully recover from something like this. All you can do is to try and cope—and go on living.

Nick, there's a certain quote that always leaps to mind when I think of you.

"Be not happy that I died but happy that I have lived."

'Til we meet again.

Your brother,

CHRIS

TO THE SUICIDAL

It Was Your Out

EMILY ANN DOWNING

Age 16, Tucson, Arizona

Dear John,

I miss you. It's been almost a year since the last time I saw you, talked to you, or even touched you. That day I found out was so horrible. I didn't believe anyone. I thought it was just a stupid joke. But it wasn't.

I keep thinking over and over in my head why you would do this to so many people that you love and who love you. But I can't think of any reasons, except that it was your out.

Others shouldn't do the same. No one wants to lose a friend, especially to suicide. They should know that there are people who will always talk to them and try to help them. There always are, always! A counselor, a neighbor, a parent, a sibling, a person on a hot line, even just a little puppy or kitten. There will always be someone there. No matter what. I'd just like all people to know that.

And, John, I'd like you to know that I miss you—so much. I just want to be able to go up to you and rub your fuzzy head and get punched in the arm again when I'm not wearing green on St. Paddy's Day. I miss that. I never thought I would, but I do.

I'll see you again, someday.

Love,

EMILY

Choosing to Die Is the One Decision That's Truly Final

RHIAN WHITE

Age 16, Willow Grove, Pennsylvania

To the Suicidal:

Don't you understand?

Why is it that you refuse to see what you have been given in life? Why do you count only what you *don't* have instead of what you *do?* I just don't understand someone who would rather die than live. Do you even have a firm belief about what happens after death? Suicide is considered wrong in any religion. Don't you see that by killing yourself, you are taking the coward's way out? Don't you realize that to stand up and say, "I am not going to let anyone or anything get me down!" takes more courage and wisdom than anything else?

There are people out there who are sick, people who are dying. Those people would give anything to have a chance to choose what they want to do with their lives. They would love to be in your position, but you don't care about that. You care only about yourself.

You don't want to look at reality. Instead you have become so introverted and so selfish that you want to die. You have given up. You *want* to take life and its opportunities away from yourself. You have decided that you never want to see another sunrise, that you never want to go for a walk on the beach or see another movie or talk on the phone or just sit outside and watch people go by. You have decided to take these things away from yourself. And why? All because of something menial. Something that you have decided you cannot take. Something that has knocked you down, and like a coward you have accepted your defeat. You have said so quickly, "I am beaten," and you refuse to get back up again.

I believe you should get back up. I believe there is always something to live for. And if you don't want to live for your loved ones or your friends, if you don't want to live for another day or another walk on the beach, then you should at the very least live because you *can*. You have been given a life and may have been placed in the position that you're in for a reason.

We've all been pushed to a place where we have wanted to give up. But part of life's challenge is to overcome the obstacles placed in front of us. How can you ever win if you decide to stop playing the game? Become someone who will be remembered fondly. Do you really want people to remember you only as someone who took their life? Wouldn't you rather be remembered as someone who was good? Someone who overcame what life threw at them and was strong?

Seriously consider your wish to die and evaluate whether you really want that wish to be granted. I hope that you find the strength to live. I hope that you can find the ability to stand up for who you are and never allow anyone else to make you feel that your life is not worth living.

Every life is precious. Everyone can make a difference. If only you would realize that just by your existence you have probably made someone's life much better, then maybe you would choose to live. Maybe you would finally understand that you are in control of your life. You decide what you believe in. You choose what kind of person you are and what morals you have.

If you would just decide to become someone who is strong and believes in themselves, you could do anything you wanted. Please don't make the choice to die. It's the one decision that is truly final.

Love from someone who believes in you,

RHIAN

SUICIDE

Dad, You Foolishly Took Your Own Life

JAMMIE SAYERS

Age 15, Thorofare, New Jersey

Dear Dad,

You foolishly took your own life. Committing suicide is such a selfish and senseless act. You don't realize what you've left behind, and those who loved you the most—those who would've helped—are left wondering what happened and why.

If only you would have spoken up, told us what was wrong, or even given a hint that something was awry, you might still be here to share your life with us.

The last thing I want to sound like is an ungrateful person, but it's hard, Dad. You weren't the father you should've been. You denied me and made me feel horrible. Still, I love you like any daughter would love her father.

And, Daddy, I miss you.

JAMMIE

"Dear Mom:

I feel the need to tell you about my experience when I was suicidal. I felt so alone in my own dark world and felt that all light had faded away. . . . What I remember intensely was that there was a terrible emptiness inside that never seemed to leave me.

Your love, in the end, was that shaft of light that saved me in my darkest hour.

I just wanted you to know."

—DANIELLE LEBLANC, AGE 17,
JACKSONVILLE, NORTH CAROLINA

"James,

I came to school that day knowing something was terribly wrong. Then Justin came and told me you had shot yourself. I never got to say good-bye, so I think this letter is my way of saying it. I pray that you will hear this:

I will love you always."

—ROBIN PETERSEN, AGE 16, PONDERAY, IDAHO

AFTERMATH OF LOSS

Jake, You're Singing with the Angels Now

JESSICA LAMBERT

Age 16, Idaho Falls, Idaho

Jake,

It's disturbing to think that I can't call you up on the phone and ask you to go skating with me. Nobody understands what it's like to deal with the death of your best friend. I try to explain that it's different somehow from losing a grandparent or aunt.

At night I stare at the stars and imagine one of them as you—looking down on me, watching over me, smiling at me. It comforts me to think that you're looking over me like you used to.

I forget you're gone sometimes, Jake. I return from work and check my e-mail and caller I.D. to see if you left a message. I become so sad when I realize that I'll never see your name on the little I.D. box ever again.

People ask me how I'm doing. I just smile and make up some excuse for why I'm not really eating. I tell them that I'm just fine, although I'm sick with grief and on the verge of tears every waking minute of the day. I wasn't surprised when my mother told me I cry in my sleep.

Each day gets a little easier. I smile a bit more, eat more, and occasionally I even manage to laugh. I try to imagine what you would have wanted me to do. I know you wouldn't want me to mourn like this, but you have no idea how impossible it is sometimes to even drag myself out of bed. . . .

Jake, you're singing with the angels now and sitting on your heavenly father's lap. Your smile will stay with me always in my heart. Your good works for people and your tender spirit will never die.

I promise never to forget and never to let go.

JESSICA

"I've decided to put all my memories in a box in my heart and start from the beginning . . . no more tears for this girl."

—DIANA COELHO DE SANTA-CRUZ, AGE 15, VILA N DEGAIA, PORTUGAL

"The world may or may not be allowed to hold us, but in my recent loss of a loved one, I start to realize that the world is not always a place to live, but a place to breathe. . . ."

—ADAM HOGUE, AGE 19, LOWELL, MASSACHUSETTS

"Loss makes people more compassionate, caring, and giving, for in loss we finally realize that nothing lasts forever, that happiness is finite, and that no one is immortal.

Loss teaches us to make every moment worthwhile and to cherish those we love because we never know how long they'll be with us. . . . "

—Irwan Kurniawan Muhammad, age 19,
Pahang Darul Marmur, Malaysia

PART FOUR

Challenges

“I’m ready to start the revolution. Call anytime . . .”

—Stacey Jowett, age 17,
Yorktown, Virginia

PART FOUR

Body Image

BEING OVERWEIGHT

EATING DISORDERS

SELF-INJURY

Substance Abuse

SMOKING

ALCOHOL

DRUGS

CHALLENGES

Body Image

BEING OVERWEIGHT

Hey, World, I'm Coming. See You Soon

VALERIE SEIMAS

Age 16, Tracy, California

Hey, world:

Most would think that I don't have anything to smile about. I'm overweight. I've never had a boyfriend. Most would say that I haven't experienced life. But I live every day with a smile and can accomplish anything I put my mind to.

So what's this letter for?

To tell you I'm coming.

One day, you're going to turn around and there I'll be—the stereotypes crashing in around us.

I'm going to be there. You might not like me. You might not want me. But I'm coming.

See you soon.

VALERIE

The Size of My Pants Makes No Difference

MANDY HARTER

Age 17, Poulsbo, Washington

Dear People:

The taunts in the classroom, the jeers in P.E., and the super-beautiful people who refused to open their eyes are not exactly my kind of pleasure.

Well, I've got news for you. There *are* people in this world who want to be with people like me. They don't all laugh and point and snicker. And they're the smart ones in life, the ones who will go on to be great professionals, wonderful parents, and reliable friends.

They realize that the inside is what matters and that the size of my pants makes no difference as to who I am as a person.

MANDY HARTER

EATING DISORDERS

My Soul Feels Empty and Desolate

ALISSA MILLER

Age 17, Lino Lakes, Minnesota

Dear Society,

I'm just an ordinary teenager, supposedly living an ordinary life. Unfortunately, I can't anymore.

My soul feels as if it has been left empty and desolate. I am haunted by the gaping ravine between the image I want to obtain and the misshapen one that appears to me in the mirror every morning.

I starve myself sometimes, refusing to feed the monster that I provide sanctuary for. Society has planted the seeds: airbrushed models, reports of looks mattering more than brains, diet commercials, and the overwhelming cultural obsession with weight.

People speak of the evils of culture, yet no one seems to have the strength to take the first step and change it. People assume that it is not their responsibility, or that they are not the ones who will suffer from the cultural obsession with weight.

I can assure you, it affects everyone, from the athlete to the prep, from the honor student to the "normal" teenager, from the captain of the science team to those who claim it doesn't affect them at all.

I beg of you, Society, do not allow us to continue to suffer from this calamity. By broadcasting this falsehood to us, you are only selling yourself a dismal future of potential leaders too obsessed with their appearance to become the leaders the world needs.

Change.

ALISSA

SELF-INJURY

I Was a Cutter

JAE CHESSON

Age 15, Fairbanks, Alaska

To the teenagers of this world who feel alone,

I was a cutter. The technical term is self-mutilation or self-injury, but you can call it whatever you want.

During this period of my life, I felt alone. I felt as though I had no one to talk to, no one to share my problems with. I couldn't tell my parents; I couldn't even tell my very best friend. Before this happened to me, I could tell them everything, absolutely everything. But it changed. I changed.

I didn't want to tell anyone. I was extremely ashamed of what I was doing to myself, though at the times when I did cut myself, I felt an amazing feeling of power, of control. But afterward I felt ashamed, guilty, and always alone. So scared, too frightened to talk, I became uncommunicative and reverted into my shell.

All of my friends were amazed yet worried, as I'd always been a fairly outgoing and happy person. My parents and teachers also noticed my sudden unhappiness but didn't push the subject, until one particular day. It was a Wednesday. For the past two nights, I had hacked away at myself, at my ankles and stomach, resulting in some fairly bad cuts. I was in social studies and was particularly quiet, even more than usual, and my teacher picked up on that. She asked me quietly at the end of the lesson if I wanted to talk, and I broke down.

I'd reached a crisis point, and the tears just wouldn't stop. I told her pretty much everything, and she almost pushed me to see the school nurse, which ended up being one of the best moves of my life. The nurse gave me some help-line phone numbers and was always there to listen. And it got better; it really did.

What's the point of this letter? It's to let you know that there is help. There is always someone willing to listen and to help. Even if you don't think your problem is that significant, there will always be someone. Schools usually have support channels, and the phone numbers of help lines are usually listed in phone books. If you are feeling depressed or worried, I hope that by reading this letter you will seek help, because then my life would be worthwhile. Even if just one person reads this and seeks help, it makes it all worthwhile.

Don't keep it inside.

JAE

> “Being fifteen isn't as fun as it's made out to be. Sure, you're young and full of energy, but inside you feel like you're just hanging on by a shred of hope.
>
> One day you can't take it anymore—the desperate feeling of trying to prove that you're worthy of people's attention. You decide to mutilate yourself, cutting up your arms, not realizing that you'll be scarred for life.”
>
> —JACLYN PEARCE, AGE 15,
> WINNIPEG, MANITOBA, CANADA

The Source of My Pain

VICTORIA MARTYN

Age 21, Eugene, Oregon

To Everyone Like Me,

Life has been really tough on you lately. I'm not sure what's going on that's making it so tough, but I know you find whatever it is horribly confusing. You feel pressured when no one is pressuring you. You feel paranoid even though no one is whispering about you. You surround yourself with morbid thoughts and feel like no one cares, and even the people who do care just don't care enough. You are second best. You are important to no one.

I went through that, too, during my first year of college. It was the first time in my life that I had left the confinement of my small Midwestern town and the comfort of my circle of friends. By some chance of fate, three of my friends were going to my college as well, and I found comfort in that. But when we got to college, they made new friends and left me in the dust. At least it felt that way.

There was one friend who stuck by my side, a boy that I had liked for four years, although I'd been too afraid to admit it to him. So I spent my time in his dorm room, staring at the picture of his girlfriend on his desk and wishing. I never even opened my eyes to any other possibility of friends or dates that might have existed elsewhere in college. I chose to live in the past and hated myself when everyone around me wanted to step into the new world around them. I merely concentrated on myself. I was never pretty enough, never skinny enough, never got enough attention. I was just not good enough.

I withdrew into myself. I began to have suicidal thoughts and spent most of my day sleeping just to avoid having to live. I began to practice self-mutilation, taking a razor blade and gashing the top of my hands and arms just hoping that someone would notice how much pain I was in, physically and emotionally.

The odd thing was, *I* was the source of my own pain in the end. *I* was the one who was secluding myself from the world and refusing to see what was right in front of my face. *I* was the one who refused to accept that I was loved, that people did care about me. And *I* was the one who was digging myself further and further into a hole, hoping that the sides would cave in so I could just give up.

I want to tell you that there is no reason good enough to make you give up. Pain is often fleeting and in retrospect can seem just plain silly. I'm not saying that your pain is false; the smallest things can cut like a thousand knives. But you—we, all of us—need to look deep within to discover the true source of the problem. I guess what I'm really saying is this: if anything is ever going to change, you are going to have to start with yourself. And change is not a bad thing. It can only lead to new experiences, and every experience is a jewel of life.

Never give up living—and I wish you the best of luck in all of your life's journeys.

With love,

VICTORIA MARTYN

Substance Abuse

SMOKING

Dear Marlboro Cigarette Company: Money or Life?

HOLLY MILES

Age 12, Calgary, Alberta, Canada

Dear Marlboro Cigarette Company:

I must say I am quite disgusted with your company. You are getting rich off slowly killing people. Cigarette smoking is addictive, and it kills. It causes lung cancer, throat cancer, and birth defects, and every cigarette you smoke takes ten minutes off your life. You know that, but you don't care. All you care about is money. What do you do with that money, anyway? Why is it so important to you? Do you value life? It's a gift you get only once. Once!

My aunt smokes. She wants to quit, but she can't. She has a son, too, and he loves her very much. And he'll have to bury her. She's smoked since she was about sixteen. If she's smoked one pack a day, she's taken around 550 hours off her life. You get rich off encouraging people to inhale stuff like tar, and yet you can still sleep peacefully at night. How? I'll never understand that.

Why do you value getting rich over other people's lives? Why can't you get rich by helping people, like owning a chain of health food stores instead of killing them by encouraging them to smoke? Who came up with the idiotic idea that people should smoke, anyway? It's disgusting, seeing people having to have holes cut in their throats so they can breathe. And still people try smoking, get addicted, and throw away their lives to be in the "in" crowd.

Please take the time to think about what you prefer. Money or life? I'll leave that to you.

Sincerely,

HOLLY MILES

ALCOHOL

I've Never Drunk Since

JEREMY COAN

Age 15, Mansfield, Texas

To Teens Who Have Driven While Intoxicated:

I have a story to tell you. I used to drink all the time—on weekdays, weekends, anytime I could. But that all changed one day after I went to a party with some good friends.

My friends got wasted and were driving home. Four of them were in the car, and Dave was driving. Dave couldn't handle the speed he was driving at, and he flipped the car six times. No one was wearing a seat belt, and all four boys were thrown from the car. Dave was killed instantly, Lance was unconscious, and

Stuart was dying on the road. Joseph was the only one unharmed, but as he tried to pull Stuart from the road, a car ran over him.

I cried for days when the police called me. I've never drunk since.

Sincerely,

JEREMY COAN

Dad, All We Share Is Silence

KELSEY SMITH

Age 16, British Columbia, Canada

Dear Dad,

I wonder if I'll ever have the guts to actually let you read this letter because in it I'm going to be perfectly honest.

When I was younger, I remember being "Daddy's little girl." You came to my soccer and baseball games, and cheered enthusiastically for me. But as I grew older, something happened. When I think of you now—of us now—my mind is flooded with images of us arguing and you trying to grasp and control my life in any way you can.

Throughout my life I've hidden the fact that you were an alcoholic for fear of being judged. To this day, I've told no one. Even though you've dealt with your addiction, I feel like you have a deeper problem to overcome.

To be perfectly clear, you make it overwhelmingly difficult to love you. I've endured your temper, selfishness, and fundamental lack of respect for anyone but yourself for sixteen years now. I still don't see how you expect me to respect you, when you obviously have no respect for me. I don't understand why you tell me not to do something and then, hypocritically, do it yourself. I hate how you treat Mom so poorly, and it hurts me even more the way she puts up with it. You epitomize the type of man I don't want to marry.

The truth is that over the last few years I've simply given up. And I guess that you and I both know it. I only hope that we overcome this chasm before it's too late.

I don't take for granted that I have a father who loves me when there are so many in this world who are fatherless. And I don't take for granted that you work and make sacrifices for my well-being.

But, Dad, you're hurting me more than you'll ever realize, and you're hurting yourself, too, in the process. Until you realize what you're doing to me and to the rest of our family, the only thing we'll share, tragically, is silence.

I'll love you forever,

KELSEY SMITH

To the Drunk Driver Who Killed My Friends

CAROLINE MASON

Age 14, Manassas, Virginia

Sir,

Hello. You may not know me, and I don't know your name. I don't know if you have kids or if you have a family. Maybe you have many close friends, but I don't, because you killed them.

Maybe you don't remember exactly what happened, but every night since you killed them, I close my eyes to try to sleep, and I see it. I see the car with my friends—they are smiling and singing like typical, happy thirteen-year-olds. Then I see your truck, and I hear a loud honking and screaming. It plagues my mind. There is blood in the car, and my friends—they aren't smiling, and they aren't singing. It's quiet now, just really silent, and then there is slamming. People slam on the brakes, they slam doors, and footsteps. Quick hard footsteps that are running, running to the car that is broken and crushed. Suddenly, everyone turns toward your truck and looks at you. Maybe the alcohol rubbed away with the stares of frightened people, but your eyes—they get big. When you start to climb out of the truck, I wake up.

You cannot deny reality. You may be sorry for every sip you took and for the lack of concern when you climbed into your truck, but you took three lives that day. Let me ask you, were three drinks worth three innocent lives? Did they do something to you? How come you climbed in that truck? Did you want to die, or did you want to live and have others suffer because you chose to drink and drive? So when you sleep tonight, clutching this letter I write you, on a cot in a room of cement and bar, you think. You think about what you did, not only to my friends but to me. About what you did to their families.

When you die and everyone is there, knowing your time is up and holding your hand, you appreciate it. My friends got cheated. No one was there to hold their hands and kiss them and tell them everything would be okay.

Goodnight to you, sir, and pleasant dreams, because I sure will never have them.

CAROLINE MASON

DRUGS

I Got Out, So Can You

DIANA EVANS

Age 18, Boulder, Colorado

Dear Brooke,

It's funny how people can know each other for so long and yet find themselves as virtual strangers. That's how I feel about you, Brooke. You feel like an unknown, like a stranger to me.

I'm writing this letter to apologize. I'm sorry, Brooke, for being so eager to jump into trying drugs that first time with you—and then that second time, and then the third and fourth times. I'm sorry that we both lost interest in our other friends, in our hopes and dreams, until eventually our lives were twisted around the one thing we thought we had going—the meth.

But you know what? What I most regret is that I pulled myself out of that trashy existence but left you there, sitting among the flies. We were best friends and were supposed to start and stop everything together. I wonder how and why everything became about the drugs when we had so much more than that.

No words can express the love that is surrounding you from your family, your friends, and from me. If you'd only reach out and touch it.

You are still my best friend, Brooke.

I'm holding your hand. I got out. So can you.

With love, always.

DIANA

"You can't leave the house without wondering what might happen today. Will my friends get high today? What will I choose to do?

These questions plague every teenager's mind.

You can't walk down the hall without getting taunted by a fellow classmate. You can't walk to the bus stop or to your car without getting asked whether you want a joint or not.

What are we supposed to do when these questions are put to us?

For me, the choice is clear: saying yes to drugs will get you nowhere."

—AMBER ZEHR, AGE 14, PONTIAC, ILLINOIS

Mom Insists She's Clean, but the Doubt Lingers

LINDSAY HAVELY

Age 14, Indianapolis, Indiana

Dear Reader:

It's weird to think that someone I knew my entire life would do hard-core crack. When Mom really got hooked, she was spending four to five hundred dollars a day on it. She cleaned out our bank account, which had all the money I had planned to go through college with. There's nothing left in it now.

I finally moved in with my sister and now avoid my mother as much as possible. Even though she is trying her hardest to stay clean and insists she is clean, there will always be that lingering doubt.

I simply can never trust her again.

LINDSAY

I Know Firsthand What Damage Drug Use Can Wreak on Families

DUSTI STONE

Age 16, Pyrorok, Oklahoma

To the World:

I'm a regular high school teenager on the outside. Inside, I have a great deal of confusion about my family.

You see, my mother is in prison for using narcotics, and it has been two years now. I've been afraid for years to confide this to my peers; I suppose I thought it would reflect negatively on me.

Eventually, I moved in with my grandmother and people realized the truth. You know, it no longer matters to me that people know because I've realized that people shouldn't judge you for anyone else's mistakes. Besides, my true friends will understand that this experience has made me a stronger and wiser person. I know firsthand what damage drug use can wreak on families, and I know never to do them.

DUSTI

Assault and Harassment

SEXUAL ABUSE

The Police Believed Him

CASSANDRA WATSON

Age 17, Midland, Ontario, Canada

Dearest Journal,

This is my first time writing. And since the bad things in my life always overpower the good things, I guess that's where I'll start.

When I was ten years old, my life became a living nightmare. It all started with this first incident, which would lead to so many others. I was involved in a club through my church, called the Pioneers Club. We did fun things, such as crafts, games, and outings. One night we went tobogganing with the club; parents were asked to volunteer as drivers and join in the fun. My friend, Tina, and I were playing with another girl's dad, Mr. Fox. We would take his hat and run down the hill. After a while, he started to get angry. Tina grabbed his hat again, threw it to me, and as I took off down the hill, he ran after me. He jumped on me, and all his weight landed on my head, crushing my neck. Luckily, I was okay. We stopped playing with him after that.

At the end of the night, everybody jumped into cars that would take them home. Tina and I were last to get there, and the only car left was Mr. Fox's. We asked our leader if we could go with him instead, but the leader assured us that we would be fine. All the other cars had already left, so we reluctantly got into Mr. Fox's car. He drove through a forty kilometer-per-hour zone going at least ninety. Tina asked him to slow down, and he suddenly squealed the car to a stop. He turned around and grabbed Tina by the neck and threatened her that she better keep her mouth shut or else. I hit his arm and told him to let her go. He did and then grabbed me by the collar instead. He swore and threatened me for about a minute. It was so scary.

When we got to the church I told my dad and we called the police. They listened to our story and listened to Mr. Fox's story.

The police believed him.

* * *

Two years later, during the summer, I would bike around my neighborhood with my dog, Duke. I always took the same route, and Duke would run alongside me. Every once in a while, Duke would run two feet onto someone's lawn and run off again. One man didn't like this; he didn't want "that dog" anywhere near his property. He started coming outside around the time I'd be biking past, and he'd watch me until I disappeared out of sight. He made this a habit.

One day as I was about to turn onto the street where my house was, I saw his car parked on the corner. I knew he had planned this to find out where I lived. Instead of biking to my house, I biked straight down to the park. He followed. He approached me in the park and asked me my name and where I lived. I refused to tell him anything. He started screaming threats and told me that he was going to find out my name and where I live and come to my house and kill me and my "stupid" dog. If he ever caught us on "his" street again, he would shoot us. He left, but I waited fifteen minutes before heading home. I told my mom and dad, and they called the police.

Once again, the police believed him.

* * *

When I was fourteen, I had my first "real" boyfriend. About three weeks into our "relationship," he came and picked me up on his dirt bike. We went down through the park and followed the trail to the piers, walked down to the water, and lay down against a tree. We started making out, but he wanted to go further. I told him I wasn't ready and that I wanted it to be really special my first time. I wanted to be in love. Isn't that every girl's dream? He wasn't convinced by my "story" and forced me to go further.

Afterward, he made me walk home as he took off on his dirt bike. I cried the whole way home and could barely walk because I was so sore. I had said "*No!*" more than once. Why didn't he stop? Why me? I didn't believe it. I wouldn't accept that I had lost my virginity so brutally.

I didn't tell anyone and just ignored his calls. About a month later, I couldn't stand it any longer; I had to know if it was true that I'd been raped. I called the Rape and Crisis Help Line and told my story to a kind lady. She answered my question simply, "Yes, you were raped."

Finally, I believed it, but I still wouldn't accept it. I kept it a secret and told only a few friends—people I knew I could trust. I wasn't ready to tell my mother, but I did tell my sister. And she cried for me and held me.

* * *

I was sixteen and starting my first job at a burger joint. I loved it until a few weeks into my job when my manager, Louis, started harassing me. He found me attractive and decided to take advantage of his seniority and my vulnerability. He started out by grabbing my butt when he walked by then poking his elbows into my breasts "by accident" and rubbing up close against me. He would make rude comments, always sexual. He would force me to kiss him, and he would feel my privates. He kept this up for five months, when he finally got fired for doing it to two other girls as well.

I decided to tell my story. I went to counseling for a few months, and then Anjie, my co-worker, and I decided to press charges. He got remanded four times then pled not guilty. I have to go to court soon and face him, his wife, and his kids.

* * *

I guess I've learned a lot from these experiences. They have strengthened me yet ruined me. These men made me afraid to love and took away my most crucial teenage years. I think puberty would have been hard enough without this. . . .

My family and friends support me one hundred percent and are very understanding. After hiding it for three years, I finally told my parents and relatives about being raped. I'm glad I didn't do it any sooner, because I just wasn't ready. Telling my family was important; it helped me to accept the fact that I *was* raped, and I can now start the healing process.

There hasn't been one day where I haven't thought about these incidents. I will have a scar for the rest of my life—a scar on my heart that keeps getting bigger. I would have preferred for none of this ever to have happened, but my mother believes that everything happens for a reason. I will try and think positively; I do believe this has made me a stronger person. And I believe God is watching over me.

Fate will take its course—

CASSANDRA WATSON

He Said That If I Told Anyone, He'd Kill Me

ANITA COLEMAN

Age 13, Salinas, California

Dear You:

When I was in seventh grade, I hung out with all of the "stoners" and "tweekers." I didn't realize what I had gotten myself into and how bad it was until something happened.

I went to a party where there were rooms—the "stoner room," the "tweeker room," the "heroin room," the "shroom room," and the "acid room." I went into every room but the heroin one. After I finished my share of drugs, I had a couple shots of vodka in the living room. I started talking to this guy who asked me to go to the store with him. I agreed, but he took me to his house instead. I went to use his bathroom, and when I came out he pushed me onto the bed and raped me. He swore that if I told anyone, he'd kill me. I cleaned up and left. I told no one.

I have dreams of this over and over and over again. It has been at least eight months since it happened. I don't hang with the same crowd anymore. And I don't do drugs.

ANITA

" Imagining my friend's pain:

I run away in my mind. My body is dead, yet he forces himself on me. My eyes remained closed, I try to think of other things—flowers in May, bunnies at Easter—but no, the pain is too much.

He hurts me, and I cry.

I think, *Why me? Why not someone else?*

After, I feel so ugly, yet I cannot hide. Everywhere I go, he is there.

I have so much hate and anger outside. Yet inside I am a child.”

—Courtney Maland, age 19,
San Luis Obispo, California

Surviving Childhood Sexual Abuse

COLLEEN STEWART

Age 17, Brewster, Massachusetts

Dear . . .

I'm not sure who to write this letter to—maybe to the thousands of men and women who share my secret. Maybe to the thousands of men and women who created this secret for all of us. Or maybe to the parents who are left in the aftermath or the siblings who are confused and often unheard because all the attention comes to us. This letter is addressed to all of the families that are devastated but most of all, I think I should address this to myself.

I am a survivor of childhood sexual abuse. I have been in therapy for it since I was three. Maybe I shouldn't write this letter, because I'm not sure I'm ready to tell as many people as will read this letter, but I feel I have to. I have been hiding this secret away for far too long, and it has affected my life too deeply to ignore it or bury it.

I am an anorexic and kleptomaniac. Both of those problems I have overcome through long, hard, painful work. My boundaries were shattered by my father, whom I don't even speak to or call "Dad" anymore, and all when I was about two. What makes these people damage a child—especially their own!—so thoroughly? I don't know, and I will never know, I guess. But I will know this—the cycle stops here.

I have enough rage inside me that I can honestly say, "No, I will not molest any child, no matter what." I will eat every day, because I will not let my father win. My body image will be shattered forever, but I will not kill myself over it. Because that is what abuse does to a child. You feel forever after that the love of others depends on how sexy and alluring you can be. How enticing you look to others. How seductive. Perhaps I will never win. But I will always try.

As I try to think of a way to close this letter, I think of all the strife my brother, who is four years younger than me, has gone through. He has been my worst enemy as well as my best friend throughout the years of guilt, anger, depression, and apathy. It has been an uphill battle, but it has cemented us together. We are friends. We are comrades. We are blood. Thank you so much, David. I love you.

Love,

COLLEEN

PHYSICAL ABUSE

He Hit Me

DANNI LUSK

Age 17, Alexandria, Alabama

Dear Momma,

Tonight I cried. I cried because he hit me. I cried because he said I was "nothing" and that I would never amount to anything in this cold, cruel world.

I cried just a minute ago, Mommy, because my heart was broken in two by words that I am beginning to actually believe. How am I supposed to know who I am other than the bad things, when all I hear is the negative?

I cried, Mother, when you held me in your arms and told me things would be okay, because for the first time I did not believe you. From then on, your "it will be okay" fell on deaf ears because reality, to me, was altered completely.

I cried until I could not breathe. I cried because every day in this country, some child is huddled in a corner, fearing for their life, just like me, and no one seems to care.

I cried tonight, while I held my baby sister in my arms. I wondered if she would have to go through the same things that we did.

I cried, Momma, when I heard your screams. I didn't know what was happening, and I was too afraid to move. All I could do was cry for you . . . and for me.

Love,

DANNI

Every Time You Beat on Me, It Kills Me on the Inside

AMANDA MACE

Age 14, Woodstown, New Jersey

Mike,

I really need to share my true feelings with you. We've been best friends for almost two years now, and most of it has been wonderful, but there have also been times when our friendship has been trying. We both have our flaws, and, granted, I have a tendency to be opinionated, but I think that both you and I realize that I'm quite a sensitive person.

Mike, I don't think you realize how much you hurt me physically, not to mention emotionally. I can take rude comments, jests, teases, and physical pain up to a point, but you always push the boundaries. We've established that you're a "button pusher" before and that you always push a little further—until I explode.

You're strong, we both know that. But you can't use your physical strength to prove your manliness! It seriously puts me in excruciating pain when you play rough. You're bigger, stronger, and taller than I am, and all I know is this: my body can't take the pain, and my heart can't, either. I guess what I'm trying to say to you is that every time you beat on me, it kills me on the inside.

I've never understood why you're so sweet to me sometimes and so violent at other times. Mike, I'm asking you with all the sincerity I have to change a little. I cherish you as a friend and would hate losing you.

Your best friend,

AMANDA

To Anyone Considering Joining the Military

SABINE E. FERRAN

Age 18, Stowe, Iowa

To Anyone Considering Joining the Military:

I was in the army for two months. It was short and far from sweet. By the end of the second week I had dislocated my knee three times and knew that I was in no condition to complete Basic Combat Training (BCT). No doctor in his or her right mind would force someone with this injury to complete something so physically grueling, but that's exactly what they did. They refused to give me a medical discharge and sent me back to training. I'm not proud of what I did, but it was necessary: I refused to train. In response, they handed me an Entry Level separation, a discharge that deducted two hundred dollars from my paycheck and prevented me from reenlisting in the military for six months.

I'm bitter that I had to refuse to train in order to get a discharge, yet even more upsetting were the scores of events that I had to experience and witness throughout the two months and eleven days at Fort Leonard Wood, Missouri. (We privates dubbed the state "Misery," for obvious reasons).

The first two weeks of Basic Combat Training, the red phase, were difficult, but they weren't as hard as I had expected. Of course, it is true that the drill sergeants play a mind game with each private—getting inches from your face and screaming at you as if you were the scum of the earth. You're never at peace—constantly having to rush from here to there, trying to complete dozens of tasks, and being punished because they're never done to the sergeants' satisfaction. I suppose I was able to cope with this because I continually reminded myself that this was just a game.

Even though I knew that the army might promote an aggressive lifestyle, it was shocking how violence-oriented army culture was. For instance, we had a session of Pugil stick training; basically, you wore ice hockey–type gear and were given life-sized Q-tips. You were then instructed to fight until your competitor was down for good. It was eerie the way drill sergeants and privates alike glowed with pleasure—urging the violence on and cheering. It reminded me of some twisted boxing match where you were supposed to hit your opponent while his back was turned or he was on the ground, begging you to stop. More than one private passed out that day.

Then there was rifle-bayonet training. This is how we had to respond to the drill sergeant:

Drill Sergeant: What makes the green grass grow?
Privates: Blood! Blood! Bright red blood!
Drill Sergeant: What's the spirit of the bayonet?
Privates: To kill! To kill! To kill without mercy!
Drill Sergeant: Who are the two of bayonet fighters?
Privates: The quick and the dead!

It was nauseating.

Would you believe that suicide attempts were not only common but unsurprising? And we actually had a riot one night; three hundred privates were supervised by one drill sergeant. The riot was inevitable and uncontrollable. Eventually, seven military police cruisers and two ambulances arrived to carry people away—either to receive medical attention or to be court-martialed.

Other aspects of the military lifestyle were equally disappointing. When we interacted with regular soldiers, they were always harried and hurried—never smiling (not proper military bearing, I guess). Benefits weren't nearly as good as the recruiters promised, either. One staff sergeant I knew earned only seven hundred dollars more than I did per month, and he had no medical insurance and had a family to support.

It might surprise you to hear after all I've written that I don't regret having joined the army. It was a tremendous learning experience, to say the least. Everywhere I looked I saw hypocrisy and isolation; no one seemed to be close to anyone else. The human touch and even a fundamental human essence was lacking. I remember feeling terrified of becoming as dull and pliant as some of the people I observed. I didn't want to lose my identity—something that seems unlikely in the civilian world but very possible in the army. After all, it's what they crave: uniformity, clones.

And I never thought I'd witness a drill sergeant coming so close to assaulting a private that he had to be restrained by his colleagues. I never thought I'd see a desperate private threaten to jump from a fourth-floor window because she had been issued a discharge and then had it revoked. I never thought I'd hear two medics debate whether to send a woman with mitrovalve prolapse back to training. And I never imagined that I'd hear a drill sergeant condone blanket parties—a sadistic ritual beating that occurs late at night among privates—and act surprised the next morning when dozens of privates were bruised and swollen.

I saw with eyes I'd never used before—eyes that got used to seeing despair and anguish on people's faces, eyes, that after nine weeks grew accustomed to seeing that pain as normal. . . . I pray that I will never have to use those eyes again.

SABINE E. FERRAN

VERBAL ABUSE

Sticks and Stones May Break My Bones, but Words Can Break My Heart

JENNIFER GEORGE

Age 16, Stuyvesant, New York

Dear Everybody,

I remember being just a little over six years old when the kids in my neighborhood decided that I deserved to be beat up. I never understood what I'd done to them; I still don't. But for some reason I was not as good as them and they needed me to know that. Every day on the walk home from the bus stop one of them would jump me so the others could hit me. After they were done, I'd sit in the road collecting my thoughts until the tears dried up. Then I'd gather my scattered books, try to wash the dirt off my face, and go home. I couldn't tell my parents. That would just prove I was a sissy.

As I got older my classmates continued to think I wasn't as good as them. In fifth grade our teacher set up a "class court" to give us a way to settle our differences without fighting. That just made it worse for me. I've always been able to deal with physical pain; it's the emotional scars that don't fade. For me, class court was unending humiliation. Every day, one of the students would take me to court for no reason (the charges were once "giving me a funny look in the hallway," as I recall), and since the rest of the kids hated me, too, I was always found guilty. I never got a fair trial. It wasn't a jury of my peers; they were all in agreement that they were better than me. The teacher didn't understand why I let it upset me so much. She used to yell at me when I wanted to cry over the trumped-up charges and cruel and unusual punishments. "Sticks and stones may break my bones, but words can never hurt me," she used to say. She didn't understand. She never even tried to.

Now I'm in high school, and a lot of the overt dislike and abuse has disappeared. I still sense the distance between myself and my fellow students, though—in the looks they shoot me across the room whenever I enter a class or the way they all flock together to one corner of the cafeteria, leaving me to eat my lunch alone; in the way I'm never chosen as anyone's partner in gym class; in the random notes of senseless hatred I find scribbled on my locker every so often. I may never understand why I'm so different from all of them, why I'm a rung below on their ladder, and I've given up trying.

All I'm trying to do now is survive.

It's hard, but I can do it. Most of the time, you can't tell how my heart is bleeding underneath the silent front I've put up for the unfeeling world. Most of the time, I seem almost normal. Most of the time.

But I never forget the one thing the world has taught me the hard way, the one thing my fifth-grade teacher never understood, and the one thing that everyone else should know:

Sticks and stones may break my bones
But words can break my heart.

JENNIFER GEORGE

Violence

"Look at our accomplishments . . . exploration, technology, medicine. Peace doesn't show up too often, though. We can sure cure a lot of diseases but can't seem to eradicate hate.

It's a plague—multiplying, spreading."

—JOSH GUENTHNER, AGE 15, IMPERIAL, CALIFORNIA

So Here's the Deal

ALECIA PEARL SAVALE
Age 13, Hartland, Michigan

Dear Youth of America:

As we all must be aware of by now, gun violence is becoming quite an issue for our generation. We have all heard about the Columbine High shootings, maybe even more than we would have liked to know. So forget about the gory details for now. Forget about the exact methods that were used by the teenage offenders, when they let go of all rational thoughts and acted out the violence they had been holding inside, possibly for their whole lives. Set all of that aside, and concentrate on *why* these occurrences have been taking place more and more. Why the ages of killers keep getting lower and the number of the victims shot to death keeps getting higher.

When I first searched for an explanation to this disturbing problem, I decided it had to be the media. I find it ironic that adults wonder why the young are losing their sanity when adults are the ones producing media for entertainment purposes that contains violent acts even worse than the Colorado massacre. What disgusts me even more is that people enjoy watching the gruesome scenes. It's really not that cool when things like this happen in reality, is it? I did research on this, yet in most of the surveys and interviews given to people our age, it has been argued that the media is indeed not to blame.

Many insist that the hate and hurt already exist in certain individuals. It has been buried in their souls since childhood, and, when triggered, it is let out on others. This leads to a new question: what is it that triggers them to let it out? In Littleton, the murderers were known as social outcasts. They were constantly being harassed by their peers. Little did their tormentors know that with every smirk, every insult that they used to entertain themselves at the boys' expense, they were adding fuel to the fire. A plot of revenge was formed and laid out for about a year, and, sure enough, it was acted upon. The result, as America now knows, was a tragedy.

Some say the parents are to blame. I do not agree. Parents can only control the actions and choices of their children to a certain extent. Many kids have worse lives at home than do the ones that murder. It would be unfair to say that parents are the reason we are falling apart.

So why do these things happen? The answer, in my eyes, is that we are doing this to one another. Imagine how wonderful the world would be if every single one of us felt loved. I'm not talking about fitting into a social group at school. I'm talking about love—the feeling that someone around your age loves you, in a friendly, "I'll always be there for you" sort of way. I truly believe that many of the problems of violence would cease to exist. This may seem impossible, but it's really not.

The stipulation is that each one of us must do our part. Let's get rid of the stereotypes. Not everyone you meet is going to be like you. We all have different backgrounds and reasons for why we are the way we are. If you torment someone, you probably have no idea what kind of emotional pain you are inflicting upon them. In fact, you are only displaying your own closed mind and your longing to fit in.

So here's the deal. The next time you find yourself discriminating against someone inside your mind and you have the urge to speak your thoughts aloud, *don't!* Even if you can't stand the person, simply keep your mouth shut. Walk away if you feel you can't control yourself.

To those of you like me who do not make fun of others, challenge yourself. Be nice to someone that you can see is having a bad day. Compliment them! If you really feel like standing out and being a well-respected person, stick up for someone who is getting harassed.

If we all do our part, this *can* and *will* stop. We need to learn now before we become adults and have to go into the real world. This will soon be *our* world. Let's not allow it to fall apart. If it does, violence among us will not seem so shocking—and that is the scariest thing of all.

Sincerely,

ALECIA PEARL SAVALE

The Media Needs to Address the Heart of the Problem

MARK PRETTI

Age 16, Ogden, Utah

Open letter to the United States:

I've been swamped with reading who the media says is to blame for the Columbine killings. It has to be Rammstein's fault, Doom's fault, their parents' fault, Marilyn Manson's fault, the government's fault, but least of all, Harris and Kleibold's fault.

Frankly, I'm not here to place blame upon anybody except Harris and Kleibold. I've always been taught to take responsibility for my actions; haven't you? So why can't the media accept that it was these two boys' own actions that left fifteen dead in Columbine High School?

In other words, perhaps the media, instead of constantly looking for a scapegoat, should go directly to the heart of the problem, which, in this case, was the *boys*—not their video games, choice of CDs, movies they watched. . . .

MARK

"There was a rumor going around my school saying that one of our students had a "list" at home that had several names on it, almost like a hit list. This frightened many students. The teachers all said it was nothing to worry about, but the students knew better. It's scary to think that the students know more than the teachers in some respects, but it's unfortunately true."

—PATRICK WAYNE BUSH, AGE 15,
NANINO, BRITISH COLUMBIA, CANADA

"There are no definitive answers as to the cause of teenage violence, but this is one teen who believes that only by thinking about these issues will we eventually learn how to prevent these tragedies from occurring."

—CODY CROSWELL, AGE 15, MILLSBORO, DELAWARE

"These days it's rough being a teenager. There's so much violence that it's sometimes hard to bear. Even in the so-called "security" of our high schools, something always happens . . .

There has got to be another way of life. Shouldn't teens feel safe and secure in school? Must we always watch our backs for attacks and assaults? Do we have to live in fear that another Columbine tragedy will occur in our own school?

Speaking as a teen myself, I feel that it all must stop before we grow up to live a life of Fear and Hate. Whatever happened to Peace and Love?"

—CASSANDRA HUBBARD, AGE 15,
CALGARY, ALBERTA, CANADA

PART FIVE

Families

“Dear Dad,

I often worry about you. Tears still come to my eyes when I speak of your heart attack. I sometimes worry that you might not live long enough to walk me down the aisle or to hold your grandchildren or to vacation with Mom after she retires. I bet you don’t know that sometimes, when you’re sleeping, I come in and check on you; I have to make sure that you’re still breathing.”

—Ellen Caton, age 19, Batavia, New York

PART FIVE

Mothers

Fathers

FAMILIES

Stepparents

Siblings

Grandparents

Parents

Mothers

Mom, What Are the Names and Ages of All Six Children in This House?

AMANDA ULVEN

Age 14, Stanley, North Dakota

Dear Mom,

I know you love me. You know I love you. But sometimes, you just explode! You have your reasons, of course. I know I can be a smart-ass, and I occasionally don't clean up after myself like I should.

And there's no denying that you've been through a lot. You had two children, lost your husband—my father. After Dad died, you made an amazing effort. We went to movies again, like when I was younger, even though you were getting less than a $100 a week sometimes and we were on food stamps. But somehow you made it all work. I still remember that you'd lie outside and we'd suntan together. You were awesome, Mom!

But after we moved back to your hometown so you could work a better job, you didn't have any time left for me. I was only ten; Steve was fifteen. It wasn't easy. Grandma sure wasn't much fun, and Steve stopped talking to me. I only saw him on his way in or out of the house.

Then you met a man, and his two kids moved in with us. Where were you when his son, a year older than me, hit me for no reason? You were sleeping because you were starting work at midnight. It was hard to feel like you weren't there to protect me.

And then I started to cry myself to sleep again, for the first time since Dad died, because Steve and your boyfriend's kids would sit outside my door making fun of me. They said I shouldn't have been listening in, but how could I not hear when they spoke so loud our neighbors could've heard?

And then you got pregnant and had a baby girl, and when you went back to work, I became her mother. I was only twelve, Mom; pushing a baby stroller around town wasn't my idea of fun. Everyone started saying that she was *my* kid. And eventually you had a baby boy. I had turned fourteen, but you thought I was only twelve.

Mom, I cook supper most of the time now. I feed your kids and your boyfriend. Your boyfriend's son helps out somewhat. Steve still doesn't talk to me. But, still, where are you?

And now I'm starting to drive, but you've only taken me out three times, once for an hour, the other two for fifteen minutes. Your boyfriend actually taught me to drive; otherwise I would have failed my test last week, or did you forget about that? You must have, because your boyfriend, not you, gave me the money for the test.

Do you remember the brown-haired girl who's almost taller than you now? "Brown Eyes," watches your kids, drives your minivan, uses your computer. You may know me only when you get a note from a teacher saying I'm doing bad in my class. Then you blow up at me, even though I've been on honors' list the whole year, and take my computer privileges away.

I have a question, Mom, and if you can answer it, I'll apologize for this entire letter. What are the names and ages of all six children living in this house? Can you tell me that?

Love,

AMANDA

You Worry That Society Will Hurt Me, Especially Since I'm an Asian Woman

SOPHIA LI

Age 14, Toronto, Ontario, Canada

Dear Mom,

You have always been the one person in our complicated family who I feel truly cares about me. It's as though your love is always circulating around me. Still, in spite of how much you love me, it doesn't necessarily mean that you understand me.

I wonder if you think that you're a fairly cool mom for a teenage daughter to have. Actually, you're not. I wonder if you realize that your style and way of life are still partially, if not entirely, ensconced in your traditional Chinese upbringing.

Mom, even though I wasn't born in Canada, I'm a one-hundred-percent Canadian teenager. I need the freedom to go out with friends without being given the third degree when I return. I need the freedom to have a boyfriend without having to keep it a secret. The shield of protection that you subject me to comes between me and my friends and will eventually be a barrier between us, too, if it isn't somewhat already.

Ever since I've become a teenager, our fights have increased exponentially. And the arguments are always the same—about me being too open with guys or something else that no other parent would consider a problem. When I try to explain that you were brought up in a different generation and that things are different you snap, "We're Chinese-Canadian, Sophia. Remember that!" And that always ends the discussion.

Still, I have to admit that you do have your cool points. I know that in your own way you try to understand that I'm a teen. You've relaxed some and now let me talk to guys on the phone. But it's not enough! I still feel trapped. Sometimes I'm so frustrated that I want to scream, and sometimes it makes me wish I had a different family.

I realize that you've created these rules for me because you worry that I'll get hurt in this society, especially since I'm an Asian woman. But, Mom, I'm not afraid to get hurt; I'm not that vulnerable! I need to have the privilege of going out by myself. That's the only thing I really want—and truly feel that I deserve.

You may never get to read this letter, but I'm going to keep trying to make you understand my needs.

I love you.

SOPHIA

One Day All the Suffering and Joy Will Meet

MAGGIE SNAPP

Age 14, Tucson, Arizona

Dear Mom,

I hurt you tonight, and there's no way I can take back the tears you shed. My own tears are welling in my eyes and heart. I'm someone you don't recognize anymore, and I can't tell you exactly what I've been feeling lately myself. What I do know is that I feel scared and lost in this unfamiliar world.

You told me I'm going through a stage, a stage that occurs in the teenage cycle. But I can't seem to categorize myself like that. I can still hear you asking me in that soft voice of yours, "Who are you?"

Mom, I don't know who I am. My life is filled with this black cloud that hovers over me day in and day out, not wanting to disappear. Does that make any sense?

I've been hurt, manipulated, and left broken by too many. My family is here for me, but I don't have the strength to turn to them yet. The only thing that gives me hope is the future. I want to know what it's like to give birth, to have a career, and to be respected. Mom, I want to participate in the world in so many ways. Someday, Mom, I'll have them listening. That's my dream.

Don't fear me, and please don't fear for me. I'll make it out of this okay, I promise, and when I make it to the other side, I'll hold your hand. Wipe away your tears, Mother, and remember that I love you and no matter what, I will become someone who will change the world.

One day I will stand next to my past and it will all come together—all the suffering and the joy will meet. And then you can say, "That's my daughter, that's my baby girl!" But until that time, allow me to grow. Allow me to experience the pain, the love, and the happiness that come with being a teenager. Together, Mom, we will take on the world!

Love,

MAGGIE

Fathers

Dad, It's Just You and Me Together as a Family

CHRISTINA MARIELLA RANDO

Age 16, Sea Isle City, New Jersey

Dad,

Sometimes I think to myself what it would be like if Mom were still around. I think that maybe things would be different, like we'd be a family again. But then I say to myself that everything happens for a reason and we'll all meet up again at the crossroads.

I remind myself that without you, I'd be nothing. You've helped me come such a long way and have encouraged me to be myself. I realize that raising me without a mother by your side must have been challenging, and I respect and love you more than you'll ever know.

Even when Mommy was sick, you stayed strong for the three of us and kept the family together. I never saw you cry until after her death, and I knew then that we needed to be strong for each other. There was too much pressure on you, and I became aware then that I also had to be there for you in your times of need. It's not a one-sided situation, you know?

You've taught me so much about life and hardships and everything in between, and I'd be lost without your guidance. I want to thank you for being a wonderful father, friend, and role model. You always know the right things to say to cheer me up, and sometimes you know me better than I know myself. I will remain grateful to you for the rest of my life, and know that I am always here for you.

And remember that when I'm in a bad mood, it's not because of you. I'm a teenager, and I'm prone to aggressive behavior sometimes. You've put me ahead of yourself so many times in so many different situations, so don't ever think that you have failed me as a parent. I don't know any other father who has gone all out for his baby girl like you have.

So now it's just you and me, together as a family. We can make this work as long as we remain headstrong. Keep your chin up, Daddy, and always hold your head high, 'cause you are really something special. Love yah!

Your baby girl,

CHRISTINA

I was Seven and Sitting Alone at a Table on Father's Day

TASMIN SCOTT

Age 15, Effingham, New Hampshire

Dear Father,

Hello. I've never met you and probably never will. But I'm your daughter, and I intend to tell you some things, even if I don't know where to send this letter. I don't know much about you, except what I've been told by Mom, and she doesn't know much either because of the circumstances that surround this. I don't know if you have any other children that you made the same way you made me. I pray you don't. I say this because it's hell—positive hell.

I've never had a father my whole life because you chose not to be present. Do you know what it's like to be seven years old and sitting alone at a table on Father's Day while all the other kids make cards for their daddies? I doubt it. But it hurts.

Even right now, after fifteen years, I can't listen to the radio and have "Daddy's Hands" or "Butterfly Kisses" come on without crying. There's another song with a line that says, "I missed her first steps, her first words, and 'I love you, daddy' is something I've seldom heard . . . watching her grow up in pictures." I used to wish that you'd do that with me. I fantasize that Mom knows where you are and that she writes to you about me and sends you pictures. I know this isn't true, but I like to dream about it anyway.

I miss the things I've never had and can only dream of. I sit on the sidelines and watch father-daughter softball games because I can't join. I wish so badly that I could. I wouldn't care if you were old and gray as long as you were mine and I could proudly say, "That's my daddy."

I've recently started dating, and I wish I had a father to bluster about and threaten to hurt my boyfriends if they hurt me. To tell me to change my clothes 'cause my shirt is too small or my jeans are too tight. There's so much I've missed and so much you've missed by not being here. I still wish you were here; I'd gladly give you a second chance, if you would just take it.

Well, Father, as I'm writing this, I'm planning on turning it in, and other people may read it. If they do, I just want to say, don't ever have a one-night stand; the consequences of it can be devastating. Remember, it's not just you that you're hurting when you have a child like that. The child will hurt more than you can ever know.

So, Daddy dearest, to what might have been. Maybe it's best left to dreams. Good-bye, Father.

Your daughter,

TASMIN

Three Little Letters, D-A-D, but to Me They Mean Nothing

JESSICA LYNN DAVID

Age 17, Langley, British Columbia, Canada

Dad,

Such a short word, *d-a-d*. Three little letters, and all I can think is that to me they mean nothing. I'm growing up now without you, just as I have for so many years. And where were you all that time? Off in your own world, I guess. I know that you and my mom don't love each other anymore, and I'm not sure you ever did, but that doesn't give you any excuse for neglecting me; it doesn't give you a free pass to Wonderland.

You know, I remember one of the worst days in my life. I was just a child, and Mom told me you were coming to visit. Dad, I was so excited. I hadn't seen you in months—I was ecstatic. So we waited and waited and waited some more. Finally the phone rang. It was you. You told Mom that a friend had called and you had decided to see him instead. I wept. But that didn't seem to affect you at all; it certainly didn't make you change your mind. I've noticed that my tears don't affect you even now; you just stare at me like I'm crazy, never offering words of comfort.

The truth is that I wish you would listen to me. I have a lot to say, Dad. But you're so closed-minded that I'm scared of what you might think and how you might judge me. It's funny, but I actually feel uncomfortable around you. You may have known me my entire life, but you don't really know me. And I still have no idea who you are, either. How much different would my life be if we lived together in the same house? Would we really talk; would you really be my dad?

Dad, this will sound harsh, but I hate you. I hate you for not being part of my life and not taking any interest in me, your daughter. I cry when I think about how you aren't a father to me.

I'm going to be someone, Dad, with or without you. But you need to make a decision and think about your priorities. If you do, you might see your daughter for who she really is—the way everyone else does—not just as an inconvenience who's costing you money.

Your daughter,
JESSICA

> "Dad, you would jump in front of traffic for me, as I would for you. You don't have the slightest idea how much I love you. And I always will."
>
> —KERRIE LYNN JACK, AGE 13, NAPERVILLE, ILLINOIS

Eugene, I Don't Really Know When I Stopped Considering You My Father

SABRINA SWEREDA

Age 14, Calgary, Alberta, Canada

Dear Eugene,

I don't really know when I stopped considering you my father. Maybe it was when you admitted that work was the most important thing in your life, or maybe it was when you neglected to inform me of my grandmother's death. Either way, you need to know how miserably you've failed me.

Before you and Mom got divorced, I thought you were the greatest dad in the entire world. That was until I noticed that you were only trying to buy my love. When I analyzed the situation, I noted that your "special outings" on weekends were usually limited to your office. I sat around and interacted with the photocopier while you made important calls around the world. You know, I really should have been doing what other kids did—playing tag at the park, throwing a ball around in the backyard, or playing with Barbie dolls.

When I was younger, I liked you better than Mom because having you around was a special occasion. I got so used to the affection and love Mom showered on me that I took it for granted. You did, too. Mom tried so hard to obey your budgetary demands at the grocery store and always had a hot meal on the table when you got home.

Thinking back to the sacrifices she made, I can hardly believe that you took off globetrotting and lied to her about your annual salary. You denied Mom the chance to pursue postsecondary education. You said she could only go if she paid the bill herself because it would interfere with your taxes. How could you have been so selfish?

Something else that I noticed was how shabbily you treated my half brother. I realize he wasn't "technically yours," but that didn't alter the fact that he needed a father. At four years old, he was certainly willing to consider you his dad. Why is it that every thought that you have is connected ultimately to you?

It's difficult to compare you to my dad now, and it's really quite amazing how much you could learn from him. Dad already had kids of his own but was willing to open his heart and welcome two more children into his life. He has done more for Mom and for this family than you ever have.

Now, with you halfway around the world, I probably won't ever see you again. Yet I hope you will, one day, open your eyes and accept blame for what you have done. Despite your beliefs, Eugene, you are not perfect.

SABRINA

To All Future Fathers

MIA WHITE

Age 17, Bloomfield Hills, Michigan

Dear future fathers of America:

Sometimes I wonder what's worse—never knowing who your father is, or knowing. For any of you who might feel nostalgia over never having had a father who was present, I'd like to share my story.

My first memory of my father is a terrible one. It was my fifth birthday, and he suddenly showed up out of nowhere demanding that I go with him. Here was a man I had never seen before, barging into my house, yelling at my mother, and demanding that I go with him. I was terrified. Who was this man? What was I supposed to do? And why did I suddenly need a father now? I hid behind my mother's leg, and when that became unbearable, I locked my bedroom until he left.

This memorable event marked my introduction to my father. Surprisingly, things weren't so volatile after that; I actually began to enjoy visiting him and my stepmother (his girlfriend at the time). My father and stepmother had children, and I was delighted to see the close bond that developed between me and my younger brother and sister.

But things started to sour as I grew older. I was always aware of my father's aggressive tendencies, but his flare-ups occurred more frequently. He'd explode at my stepmother and blame her for any inadequacies or misbehavior in the children.

My stepmother told me that he "walked on eggshells for me" to keep me happy, which puzzled me. I mean, instead of telling me what was on his mind, he'd scream at my younger siblings when he was upset at me. It was intolerable and I couldn't take it. I regularly went home in tears after every weekend I spent at that house.

Things degenerated even further. My father began showing up two hours late to meet me or would sometimes forget altogether. He never came to any of my softball games or to my concerts, and when I decided to join the cheerleading squad, he informed me that he didn't want me to become "a slut." I started getting accustomed to the disappointments and the insults.

Things simultaneously worsened at his house. I worried, and still do, for my brother and sister. He was rarely at the house when I came to stay for the weekend, and when he was there, he was usually slamming doors or yelling. Everything unraveled on New Year's Day when I was fifteen. He came home drunk and was physically unable to take me home. I won't mention the events that transpired; all I need to say is that we haven't spoken since.

So, ten years after popping into my life, he disappeared just as quickly, and since that one night, he has not called, written, contacted me—nothing. He missed my sixteenth birthday, Christmas, and all the rest of the holidays. He wasn't there for any of my award ceremonies, and I don't expect him at my graduation. For a while, he refused to pay medical bills and child support, and he has caused me, my brother, and my sister great pain.

I have had to come to terms with the fact that I no longer have a father. I do not feel like he loves me or desires any relationship with me. I know it's not my fault, but I can't help wondering why he abandoned me. Wasn't I good enough for him? How can a father just dismiss one of his children like that?

You who are reading my letter—my testimonial—may wonder why I have shared my experience with you. I will tell you why. I am seventeen years old, and I do not have a father. I have suffered immense pain, anger, and depression. My father broke my heart. I am begging you, pleading with you, not to do this to your children.

Fathers and fathers-to-be, despite the statistics about single mothers, it's still overwhelmingly difficult to grow up fatherless. The mother and father are the first loves of a child. They set the example and the standard. Think about what kind of example you set. If you don't want your child to emulate you, how can you change yourself?

Do not abandon your child. It's one of the most damaging things you can do. I have friends who have no idea who their father is, and that's a grim reality. But I will tell you, I think it's preferable to never know the man than to be rejected by him. I have no relationship with my father, and I do not desire one.

Please take what I have shared to heart, and don't let this happen to you and your children. It will leave their lives in shambles.

Your children need you.

MIA

Stepparents

Though We Are Not Related by Blood, We Are Related by Our Hearts

JAYME BLUME

Age 17, Bellevue, Nebraska

Dear Loreen,

They say blood is thicker than water, but, frankly, I know better. Though we aren't biologically related, I'm a part of you and you're a part of me. You have loved me continuously and been there for me through both good times and bad. You've listened to my problems and been a shoulder to cry on and have always, always kept my secrets.

You've never matched the evil stepmother stereotype. In fact, you're the opposite, and if I had to choose a stepmother, it would be you. Truly, you have been a blessing to this family.

Of course, we've had our arguments, but they've always ended in a hug and with an "I love you." And when I haven't learned a lesson the first time, you're patient and believe that I'll be wiser the next time around.

You've also always supported me, no matter what I do. When I quit playing volleyball and began cheerleading, you understood. When I stopped cheerleading to play soccer, you backed me up. And now that I'm changing my mind on which major to pursue, you're helping me to make the right decision.

Even when I started writing poetry, you encouraged me without being critical. I actually wrote a poem for you—two of the lines read:

Though we are not related by blood,
We are related by our hearts . . .

Loreen, I'm sorry that you never had the opportunity to have your own children, but I want you to know that I love you very much and consider myself your daughter.

With much love,
JAYME

Initially, I Didn't Want to Be Under the Same Roof as You

CHARLENE INGRAM

Age 14, Escanaba, Michigan

Dear Stepfather:

Well, it's been about five years since you married my mother. I have to admit that at first I wanted to move out and never see you again. It wasn't you—it was me. I thought you were tearing our family apart.

Through the years, I've observed how different you are from my biological father. You're much stricter, and you keep to your word. From that, I've learned to respect you.

Initially, I didn't want to know you or be under the same roof as you or want my mother kissing you. I suppose I wanted our original family to be together again. But I eventually realized that couldn't be. Perhaps there wasn't lasting love between my parents. When I was old enough to know, they told me that they had stayed together for nineteen years for us, their children. They didn't want to subject us to the kinds of changes and confusion that occur with split families. I remain grateful for that.

Anyway, I would like to thank you for being a good role model—for being the strong one when everyone else seemed weak. You've always helped us in difficult times and looked out for us when you didn't have to.

The reason I've been able to trust you is because my mother loved you. I knew that if she loved you enough to bring you into our lives, she must have known what she was doing.

And she did. Thanks, Mom!

Much love,

CHARLENE

"Father,

I have a dad now. A dad that does everything for me, and as much as I hate to say it, that's not you. You were never there for me. Yeah, you are my biological father, and I can't change that. But my dad is everything to me, and he didn't turn his back on me when things got rough, and he won't turn his back on me if things get rough again. He is there for me."

—DANIELLE DUFOUR, AGE 15, SIDNEY, NEW YORK

"Dad, even though you aren't my biological father, you'll always be my daddy. I know I wasn't easy to deal with, but you raised me like your own and made sure I never felt unloved. I couldn't ask for a better father. Thank you for giving me your name and your love. You've made me proud to be a Morales."

—Arlene Morales, age 18, Metairie, Louisiana

Siblings

My Brother, Ray, Has Undergone Three Open-Heart Surgeries

HEATHER SMITH

Age 12, Mount Marion, New York

To anyone who has a family member with medical problems:

My name's Heather Smith. During the twelve years I've been alive, my older brother, Ray, has undergone three open-heart surgeries and endured many other medical procedures.

During the long days that Ray was in the hospital, I would spend much of my time with my father and grandmother.

Praying was one of the things that helped me the most because I could feel that God was with me.

Ray sometimes got these "funny feelings," and when he did, his heart would beat over two hundred times per minute. I felt so anxious when this happened; I thought I might have to spend another night at home—frightened for Ray. Once, on Christmas Eve, Ray got a funny feeling. We filled the bathtub with cold water at midnight because the coolness sometimes helped to slow his heart down. I got upset that night. I wasn't mad at anyone, just upset. I thought, "Why did it have to happen tonight? What if I have to spend Christmas alone with my grandma and uncle?" Sometimes, though, I was able to help. During the summer, for instance, I'd get in the pool and float around with Ray.

When you have a brother or sister who isn't capable of doing everything you can, it seems that they're the ones getting all the attention. At times I've felt like I was being left out and not included; I think we all feel like that every now and then.

At these times, I think it's important to reflect on how lucky we are. Lucky that those who love us are able to rely and count on us. Lucky to be able to be inspirations to the people who need us.

Speaking of inspirations, Ray has really been one to me. He's taught me what it takes to be happy and how to tackle every day with courage and strength. I'm thankful for him and my family—especially my father, who has always been such a comfort to me. And I am so thankful to God, who helps me with all things.

HEATHER SMITH

Grandparents

Picking Strawberries Together on a Bright, Early Summer Morning

EMILY DEBELIUS

Age 15, Darnestown, Maryland

Dear Grandmother and Grandfather,

It's strange—I've often reflected about what I'd say to you if I ever had the chance, but now I'm not sure where to begin.

First of all, I want to thank you. Though both of you died before I was old enough to eat solid food, you made a significant impact on my life. Thinking of you—and the hardships you faced—has guided me and has helped me deal with various problems in life, like feelings of loneliness.

The truth is, I've always felt that both of you are here with me, in spirit and in my mind, even if you're not physically present. Thoughts of you have made me happy and wiser; they've also made me curious and sometimes have made me cry. All of these emotions are responsible for making me who I am today, and for that I will always be grateful.

I actually know remarkably little about you. What I do know is compiled from my father's, his sisters', and his brothers' memories. Even though I've heard all these things about you both, at times I feel as though I have no sense of you at all. I mean, I don't know your happy moments, your hardships, your failures, or your successes firsthand.

And while these things are important, they don't bother me half as much as not knowing the little details. For instance, I don't know what color eyes you had or the tone of your laugh. I'll never know how it feels to hold your hand or to hug you. I'll never know your smell or the kind of perfume or cologne that you wore or whether you liked lima beans or what section of the newspaper you read first in the morning. These seemingly mundane details become so familiar that people might not realize how incredibly important they are.

Grandfather, do you remember that video of you and me when I was only a few weeks old? You were bouncing me—a chubby, bald baby—on your knee and telling me that when I was older we would go to the country and pick strawberries from the orchard together. Who knew that in a matter of months you'd be gone?

When some people hear that story, they find it sad, but I, oddly enough, think it's comforting. And the reason is simple enough. Grandfather, I know that we will always be picking strawberries together, on a bright, early summer morning.

EMILY

Grandfather, See You in a Few Decades

ROBYN JOYCE

Age 17, Nelson, British Columbia, Canada

Dear Grandfather,

Even though you may be physically unable to read this, I still feel like I can reach out to you through the connection of our two spirits. In a way, I suppose these words are yet another step in the healing process we all must undergo when coping with the loss of a loved one.

The day you left us was one of the hardest days in our family's history. It's amazing how one man could have had such a giant impact on so many people's lives. At the age of sixty-nine, you seemed too young to go.

Do you remember my good-bye? I told you that I loved you, and you squeezed my hand, even though you were supposedly unconscious. That was the day I held your hand until, ever so gently, you fell asleep. But you never woke up again.

I miss you very much, and I love you.

See you in a few decades,

ROBYN

Parents

Mom and Dad, I Can No Longer Be Silent

ANGELA DONOUGHE

Age 15, Thomson, Georgia

Dear Mom and Dad,

I don't feel that you know me or have ever really tried to. If you don't recognize your daughter through these words, I'm not surprised.

From childhood on, I've always felt tremendously lonely. I don't feel like I really understand the experience of being loved because you never expressed it in the ways that conventional parents do. Mom, you never understood my attempts to get your attention, and, Dad, whenever I tried to get to know you, you were too busy watching the headline news on CNN.

I'm writing this for one reason: I need someone, even if it's not either of you, to understand how I feel. I can no longer be silent.

Sincerely,
ANGELA DONOUGHE

"My only message to parents is this: let your teenagers think for themselves; they may actually make a few good decisions on their own."

—KRYSTAL HATHAWAY, AGE 18, PINELLAS PARK, FLORIDA

Here's What Parents Should Know: Believe It or Not, We Do Try

JESSICA RICHEL

Age 15, North Tonawanda, New York

Readers, what's the deal with our parents?

I know they want the best for us, but the same old lecture, "When I was your age," can become a little mind numbing. Here's a little reality check. It's the new millennium. It's not the same day and age as when our parents were "our age."

Here's what our parents should know: believe it or not, we do try. We try our best to do what we think seems right. It's just that we have so many more problems to face each and every day, and it's impossible to always do the right thing.

Please understand that we're trying.

With all of my concern,

JESSICA

Conclusion

It seemed only natural that we would slip back into our own adolescence as we pored over the thousands of letters we received. Every time we sat down to edit, one of us would invariably end up exclaiming, "That happened to me, too!" or sighing, "I can't believe it's still like this." Working on *The Secret Life of Teens* has enabled us, the editors, to revisit our own adolescence. We realized that in our teens, charged intensity was often coupled with unrelenting boredom, and bridging the chasm with adults seemed impossible. Perhaps Jaclyn captured it best: "Life is so complicated when you're a teenager; everything seems so distant, like no matter how hard you strive for something, you can never reach it. At least that's how it feels to me." Actually, for teens, this is how it seems to feel.

OUR ROLE AS ADULTS

After reading thousands of letters from the real experts in this generation—the young themselves—we are convinced that this generation will surprise you. Indeed, William Strauss, coauthor of *13th Gen* and *Fourth Turning*, similarly predicts that these teens will be awe inspiring. In his words, "They will be the heroes. You watch. At the turn of the millennium, magazine covers will be proclaiming that they are a wonderful generation."

They've already made it abundantly clear that with or without adult support, they're coming; as Valerie states, "One day, you're going to turn around, and there I'll be—the stereotypes crashing in around us. I'm going to be there. You might not like me. You might not want me. But I'm coming. See you soon." And Jaime says equally directly, "We persevere in a world that doesn't want us. We will strive and rise like the Phoenix out of the fire with more knowledge and experience than any other generation in history."

Perhaps what surprised us most was when these teens confessed to feeling discarded, like an unwanted generation. As adults, we know this isn't true; not only are they wanted, they're cherished. And we can no longer accuse them of not doing their part! The thousands of teens who contributed to this book surely represent the majority of young people who want to communicate with us adults.

Now, it's our turn—our turn to make a concerted effort to hear what this generation is really saying to us. And should we forget to listen to their stories—instead of telling them ours—we can keep these words, courtesy of Steffanie, in mind: "*Just because you were a teenager doesn't mean you understand*." Or to paraphrase Jessica, "Here's a little reality check. It's the new millennium. It's not the same day and age as when our parents were 'our age.' Here's what our parents should know: we do try—each and every day—we try our best and will keep on persevering."

The time for adults to meet this generation halfway has arrived, and we better act now because it won't last for long. The teen years are a crucial time—some suspect the last time—when they are still flexible enough to be willing to listen openly and to be vulnerable. What's wonderful is that this generation is providing us with clear instructions and specific ways to help bridge the gap. In Stacey's words, "Eventually, the future will become the past and the children of today will become the leaders of tomorrow. We will be presidents, senators, mayors, and some of you will be gone. We will be great men and women, World, but not if you don't help us. We need you to talk to us . . . as if you are equals to us. World, we can be all that you want us to be and more. Just give us a chance. Help us out a little. And we'll handle the rest."

Think about it.

To Contact the Coeditors

If you'd like to reach the coeditors, Gayatri Patnaik and Michelle T. Shinseki, or contribute a letter for their future projects, please write to them in care of their publisher, HarperCollins.

Gayatri Patnaik & Michelle T. Shinseki
c/o Author Mail, 7th Floor
HarperCollins Publishers
10 East 53rd St.
New York, NY 10022

Or, visit their web site at www.secretlifeofteens.com.

Index of Names